BIRD DOCTOR

BIRD DOCTOR

by

KATHARINE TOTTENHAM

THE COUNTRY BOOK CLUB
LONDON 1963

CONTENTS

LIST OF PLATES

between pages 102 and 103

CHAPTER ONE : A SEA OF TROUBLES

IT was a moment of real excitement for me when I opened the basket containing what was supposed to be a sick kittiwake and found a large gull-like bird, emitting harsh croaks from a hooked bill surmounted by bluish tube nostrils, and glaring with a pair of black eyes glamorously fringed with dark hairy feathers. Without doubt a fulmar.

In global terms, fulmars exist in such vast numbers that they are close to being one of the commonest birds in the world ; yet for someone living in southern England they are a comparative rarity and of the greatest interest.

Fulmars, with two petrels and three shearwaters, are the representatives in our waters of the family of sea birds known as tube-noses. Until the latter part of the nineteenth century the only British fulmar colony was on St Kilda, where they nested in enormous numbers in spite of depredations by the islanders, who extracted the large amount of oil secreted by these birds, ate the carcasses, and used the feathers for bedding. Since then, fulmars have spread steadily southwards and now are found prospecting for nest sites off the coast of Cornwall, and have established small colonies on the Atlantic and extreme south-west coasts of Ireland.

My fulmar was so weak that it was forced to rest on its elbows, but it was still full of fight. Rather like a skunk in reverse, the fulmar's most effective weapon is a jet of foul-smelling yellow oil which is fired from the open gullet with unpleasant accuracy ; a knack for which, as far as I know, it can claim exclusive rights. After several tentative overtures, the resulting douches of oil and a complete change of clothing, sterner methods were obviously demanded, and as it gaped I put a finger crossways into its bill.

Apart from the hooked tip, a fulmar's bill is fairly soft, to match its diet of small jelly-fish, plankton, offal from whaling-ships, and an occasional fish. The hooked part, as in shearwaters and petrels, is only used on the bird's annual trip ashore for nesting, when it is employed as a sort of alpenstock.

Once gagged, my fulmar relaxed and allowed itself to be examined for injuries. There were none apparent and it seemed likely that the only trouble was malnutrition ; certainly there is no waste blubber in the neighbouring sea. The job then was merely a matter of feeding, but on what ? Plankton was out, the arrival of jelly-fish on the shore is spasmodic, and fish are no more than a side-dish in fulmar gastronomy. Oily matter, the books said, and so the first experiment was with sardines, and to my relief these were taken eagerly. Herring strips soaked in cod-liver oil added variety, and meanwhile a band of youthful jelly-fish spotters were recruited in the village. I insisted on reports only, fearing the chance of enthusiasts gathering armfuls of Portuguese men-of-war, and after two days was told of a jelly-fish stranded on the sands.

I found a monstrous object, big enough to fill a two-gallon bucket, and staggered bravely home with it, faced with the job of carving suitable slices for the fulmar's supper. I have rarely undertaken a more repulsive task but it was well rewarded : from then on the bird began to recover and was able to stand firmly on its legs.

Searching every possible source of information, I found a note in an old book saying that tube-noses often ate sorrel while on land and that this plant possibly had medicinal properties for the birds. Reference to John Gerard's *Herbal* told me that sorrel will . . . *refresh the spirits overspent with the violence of furious or fiery fits of agues, . . . quench thirst and . . . procure an appetite in fainting or decayed stomachs, for it resisteth the putrefaction of the blood, killeth worms and is a cordiall to the heart.*

Extracting and condensing this somewhat dramatic account of its remedial qualities, the plant appears to be a general tonic and vermifuge, which might be useful. I picked a bunch and offered it to the fulmar, who immediately began stripping the pods with its bill and swallowing them with evident relief or pleasure. The combination of jelly-fish and sorrel were the makings of a new bird, and the real beauty of a fulmar became apparent.

It is slightly larger than a kittiwake and smaller

than a herring gull ; the mantle, wings and tail blue-grey, and the remaining plumage a yellowy white. In fact, I think the white is pure white, but in preening, a certain amount of yellow 'stomach-oil' is secreted to stain the feathers. The legs and feet are again rather gull-like but pale blue in colour, and the webbed toes are armed with sharp claws. In common with most oceanic birds, fulmars are not agile on shore and tend to shuffle about in a manner quite unlike the strut of a gull.

This fulmar was not the first sea bird to convalesce in our kitchen. Storms make a beachcomber's paradise of the sand and rocks that line the stretch of Devon estuary where I live : timber and kindling-wood ; tins of ships' biscuits, perhaps from a merchant-man sunk with all hands, but more probably cast overside by some frustrated sea cook ; a dead seal and a pathetic bloated body that was once a pig ; and after the worst gales or the release of waste oil from a passing ship, dead or barely alive sea birds litter the tide-line or hide themselves among the rocks.

Many who survive the waves fall victims to a band of hungry crows ; a few we find and bring home for treatment, although, like the fulmar, the majority of my patients now arrive second-hand from all over the west country.

It was soon after we came to live by the shore that my Labrador brought me the first of the many bird visitors, a wigeon duck wounded by gunshot in the wing. She soon settled down in a chicken coop with a wire-netting run on the lawn, but we were faced with the desperate problem : what would she eat ?

Like domestic geese, wigeon are grazing-birds and formerly fed almost exclusively on the marsh weed *Zostera*. Some years ago an epidemic blight largely destroyed this plant, leaving vast flocks of wigeon and brent geese foodless, and as a result their numbers decreased alarmingly. Then, like the buzzard when myxomatosis wiped out its natural diet, the survivors began to eat other types of food : vegetation and some animal matter including small fish, insects and worms.

On this basis, feeding my wigeon duck should have been comparatively simple, but layers' mash was rejected with contempt, so was water-weed and green seaweed ; boiled corn, no ; and no to any form of domestic duck food, worms, small fish, and smashed-up snails. Then, by chance, I got it : bread and milk and grated cheese—simple enough if one was not so hide-bound as to expect a wild duck to be conservative in taste.

On this diet she thrived ; taking extremely noisy baths in a wash-hand basin at midnight and sunning herself all day, until after a month or so she recovered her strength, though it was apparent that she would never fly again, the shotgun pellets having in effect pinioned one wing. Inquiries at a zoo brought the eager reply that a bachelor wigeon drake was in residence, and so she went off to join him on a large pool with several mandarins and Carolinas, which must have amazed her with their tropic colouring.

In those days I was not equipped to look after wild birds for any length of time, and so sadness was mingled with relief when she was gone ; but hardly a week passed before another visitor arrived : this time a young and hungry herring gull, again with an injured wing. Food was no problem here, just pound upon pound of sprats ; the only proviso being that they must be fresh—no garbaging for this gull.

He was allowed the freedom of our back garden, where he remained aloof except at feeding-time ; then he came at a shambling run to snatch a sprat or two, rudely, before returning to contemplate space from a hillock of grass. This somnolence was only interrupted by baths and, more occasionally, by an odd little dance, which was executed in one spot—a habit that puzzled me for some time until I came across a reference to it in a book, the author supposing that the drumming of the bird's feet on the sand might suggest to some foolish lugworm that the tide was in and that it was safe for it to poke out its head.

Alas, poor Albert Herring was no better after three months, and so I gave him a sudden end. My knowledge of first-aid for birds was very threadbare then ; now I would know that he was beyond help from the beginning.

But by then an unwarranted local reputation had been established and brought several more casualties : a smart, red-legged, black-headed gull, who recovered and was released at a reservoir to gain strength before returning to the sea ; and many others which lived or died according to their will, the seriousness of their injuries or oiling, and my capacity to understand them.

And then came a real challenge, a wild thing of the wild seas, a Manx shearwater. Few people, apart from fishermen and sailors, have a chance of seeing these birds, which spend most of their lives well beyond the three-mile limit, only venturing ashore on rocky islands or the most inaccessible parts of the coast, where they breed in old rabbit burrows.

My shearwater had got into an oil slick, to be covered from head to tail in the thick tarry horror. Unable to fly or to swim, it was cast ashore in a bay farther up the coast and picked up by a party of Cockney holiday-makers who, with some remembrance of having read somewhere the treatment for oiled birds, washed it in warm detergent suds and smothered it in lard (the reverse of the procedure recommended at that time). They fed it sips of brandy and bits of bully beef and, when I met them, were distractedly trying to persuade the poor bird to fly away as they had to catch a train home.

My offer to take over the job was warmly welcomed, but at first I had slim hopes for the bird's survival ; for though it was free of fuel oil it was now matted in lard and very weak. I wrapped it in a bed of warm hay and forcibly fed it with slivers of raw fish dipped in cod-liver oil, until gradually life began to return.

2

After a few days the lard wore off and I found a beautiful creature beneath ; black and white and resembling a large swift, but with a long, tube-nosed bill hooked at the tip, and pink-and-black webbed feet ending in hook-like claws. To start with, I put its complete tameness down to exhaustion ; but as the days passed and it became more and more lively, it was obvious that its friendliness was natural : its forebears had nothing to fear from man, or any terrestrial animal for that matter, and it was as tame as an Antarctic penguin.

We have five dogs, two of which are large, but all fortunately accustomed to putting up with odd pets about the house, for the shearwater took to them at once and would plod about the kitchen floor regardless of human or canine feet, peering up in hopes of a titbit. Fish of various kinds was its sole diet and this had to be fed by hand, as these birds naturally dive under water or snatch from surface shoals on the wing, and have no idea of picking up still food from a dish.

The flight of a shearwater is fast, and it has the habit of tilting from side to side as it travels over the surface of the sea, often scything through wave tops with a wing tip and thus gaining the descriptive name. Like the auk family, it also ' flies ' under water, using its wings as oars while the webbed feet paddle behind like an outboard motor.

It is a great climber, using its bill and claws, and my one would laboriously clamber up the side of the
(2,343)

sofa to balance on the arm and flutter its wings like an electric fan.

These birds, again like swifts, have great difficulty in taking off from a flat surface, and for this reason are provided with hooks to enable them to climb high rocks from which to launch themselves into the air. Once airborne, however, they will travel immense distances and think nothing of crossing the Atlantic, even venturing to South America.

My shearwater was soon fit enough to fly, but two problems remained : the first was that gulls are the main enemies of the small petrels and shearwaters, which they tend to mob and kill on sight, and so there was the difficulty of finding a gull-less part of the coast for the release. The second problem then proved insoluble, for I had come up against ' wet-feather ' for the first time, though I had no idea that this was what it was called. I thought that using the detergent directly on to the feathers instead of on a basis of lard had removed all the bird's natural plumage oil, and that this was why it was no longer waterproof or buoyant. Certainly it was obvious that if I released the bird in this condition it would fly far out to sea and sink like a stone the moment it settled on the water. All I could do was to wait and hope that the oiliness would return in time.

My previous experience with various kinds of sea birds seemed to provide evidence of a definite pattern in their recovery.

At first it was touch and go whether they lived or

died ; then they seemed to decide on living and began preening themselves and became interested in food ; from that stage convalescence went forward steadily towards a peak, and when they reached that peak the crucial time was near. All being well, they could be released to return to their natural lives, but if for some reason, as in the case of the herring gull and the shearwater, they were unable to go, then they were liable to go downhill rapidly and die.

I believed that the cause must be some deficiency in the diet obtainable perhaps in sea water or plankton. Whatever the answer, the same obviously did not apply to land birds, which usually settle down quite well under domestication.

The shearwater followed the pattern, growing steadily stronger until the balance tipped and one day I found it dead.

That year I looked after nine birds, and more than half of them recovered and were released ; but the majority were perching birds, either fledglings or adults, with minor injuries. The following year the number of birds doubled and my successes dropped to forty per cent, and the reason for this was oil. Those pages of the register I keep of all the birds treated make sad reading :

Kittiwake		*died*
Manx Shearwater	2—	*died*
Guillemot	2—	*died*
Herring Gull	2—	*died*
Gannet		*died*

is that all appears on the sea-bird section ; and that is what drove me to specialise in the study of oil pollution and its effect on some of our most beautiful birds.

I began with a programme that concentrated upon badgering individuals and bodies who might provide possible sources of information, and during this search I obtained valuable advice from the R.S.P.C.A. ; the Royal Society for the Protection of Birds ; the International Committee for Bird Preservation and its Co-ordinating Advisory Committee on Oil Pollution of the Sea ; and from the American naturalist Frederick C. Lincoln, who took the trouble to have a photostat copy made of his paper addressed to the North American Wildlife Conference for 1936, in which he detailed the effect of oil pollution on wild-fowl in the United States at that time.

Added to this, I collected individual views from various naturalists and from Royal and Merchant Navy sailors, and the result was a thick folder containing almost every known fact about this terrible subject.

The history of serious oil pollution affecting water-fowl began some thirty years ago when more and more ships were equipped with diesel engines. In 1928 the steamer *Robert E. Lee* sank off the coast of Massachusetts, releasing a large quantity of oil which caught a mass of wildfowl in the midst of migration. Within a few days the beaches north of Cape Cod were covered with thousands of dead and dying duck.

From time to time equally large numbers are gathered in places all along the United States eastern seaboard.

More recently, Britain had an example of the effects of oil pollution : more than five hundred Thames swans became soaked and helpless when the tanker *Stoneheath* sank in Elms Reach. This disaster focused public attention on the horrors of pollution, as sightseers and pressmen crowded wharfs and docksides to watch R.S.P.C.A. workers fighting to save a proportion of the swans.

A year or so later the scene shifted to the Baltic, where a rogue vessel illegally dumped waste oil and killed some thirty thousand sea birds.

However, not all the blame for oil pollution lies at the doors of industrial and shipping interests. The terrible decimation of ships in the submarine warfare of World War II has left a legacy of sunken tankers lying beneath the Atlantic, many with their keel tanks still unbroached. Immersion in water slows the process of rusting considerably, and it is estimated that fifteen to twenty years may be needed before sea pressure finally bursts the steel casings to release hundreds of gallons of imprisoned oil, which gouts to the surface and spreads over an area of several miles, running like quicksilver to form tarry masses and voyaging along the nearest current, carrying impartially a cargo of weed, wreckage and sea birds.

Even so, spillage by passing ships is still largely responsible for the pollution of our seas, and at intervals conferences have been called by interested governments, and proposals put forward at various international meetings, but total agreement has never been reached ; indeed, it was not until 1953 that a solid foundation was laid for the outlawing of oil spillage on the high seas. This was at an unofficial conference organised in London by the British Co-ordinating Advisory Committee on Oil Pollution of the Sea and attended by representatives of twenty-eight countries.

The following year, forty-two nations were officially represented at a similar meeting and adopted a convention which, when ratified, would prohibit the discharge of persistent oil into the sea except in certain agreed zones.

In the case of Britain and the countries bordering the Channel, North Sea and Baltic, this, it was hoped, would provide almost complete isolation from the dumping-zones, and the incidence of oil on our beaches would become a rarity.

Meanwhile, a passing tanker dumped six thousand tons of crude oil into the North Sea, causing havoc along our south-east coast ; and on the beaches of Sussex and as far west as Cornwall oil sludge gathered in such quantities that lorries were employed to remove it and armies of charwomen spent the early-morning hours scrubbing pebbles at the expense of seaside town councils.

Then, five years after the initial London meeting, the International Convention came into force on 26 July 1958, ratified by eleven nations—Britain and the Irish Republic, Denmark, Norway, Sweden, Germany, Holland, Belgium, France, Mexico and Canada. A few months later Finland followed suit.

But, splendid as this advance was, it still left half the world's shipping tonnage, including that of the United States and the suppliers of flags of convenience —known collectively as Pan-Hon-Lib—at liberty to spill waste fuel oil anywhere on the seven seas outside the immediate territorial waters of the twelve signatories.

The vagaries of ocean currents sweep insoluble oil at an average speed of ten miles a day from mid-Atlantic towards the British Isles and Western Europe, or upwards to pass below Greenland and pollute the shores of eastern Canada. In Britain the south-west coast is often the landfall of oil from the Atlantic, which carries with it a toll of dead and crippled birds : shearwaters, scoters, guillemots and razorbills are the commonest victims, but other sea and estuary divers crop up occasionally, including cormorants, grebes, great northern and red-throated divers, as well as various sea-going duck.

Autumn and spring bring in the largest number of birds, some presumably caught on migration and others perhaps jeopardised by special habits during the winter and summer plumage moults.

In the majority of cases the oil attaches itself to the lower breast and tail regions on a bird, and I suspect that in some instances this may be due to a last-second effort on the part of the victim when it is surfacing from a dive and sees above it the dark ceiling of oil slick. If it were then to throw itself backwards in an attempt to crash-dive once more, the impetus might sweep the belly and tail along the underside of the oil before the bird had time to generate enough power to force itself downwards and out of danger. But this may be a fanciful view, and perhaps it is merely the bow wave of a floating bird that pushes the oil to the rear before it can stick.

Sometimes the all-pervading oil smothers the whole bird and then its death is mercifully quick, though none the less grisly. I shall not forget the spectacle of a solidified sheet of oil lying on the sands, and within it, as if carved in bas-relief, the outlines of a spread-eagled duck.

While the many dead and dying birds are testimony to the outrage of pollution, my concern was with the few who come ashore alive. My inquiries had produced plenty of information on the cause and immediate effect of oil pollution, and the R.S.P.C.A. had a store of knowledge gained from experience of the care of swans, but sea birds are different in many ways and remained largely an enigma.

Swans, though subject to chilling and subsequent pneumonia, remain buoyant in all circumstances and will not drown if they are oiled ; but if the water-proofing system of sea-bird plumage is damaged to the smallest extent then buoyancy automatically breaks down and the bird's natural element becomes an enemy bent on destruction. With this in mind

it is easy to understand the pitiful condition of the
birds that do come ashore.   The oil is the root cause ;
physical exposure and mental bewilderment and stress
are the lethal secondary factors that kill many rescued
birds.   This psychological aspect adds immeasurably
to the complexity of bringing the birds back to a point
where they are fit to return to their natural lives.

CHAPTER TWO : TURN OF THE TIDE

THE time lag between initial oiling and a bird's arrival for treatment is a yardstick for its chances of survival, because a cold and wet sea bird, suffering from starvation, is a sure candidate for pneumonia unless food and warmth can be provided within an hour or so.

People who find oil victims are naturally horrified by the crippled state of these once beautiful birds, and expect me to perform a miraculous cure ; but more often than not the rescued one is beyond help.

A tragi-comic example was the soldier who stood on the doorstep, in immaculately pressed battledress, gaiters and gleaming boots. He gave me one of those flat-handed, quivering salutes and said, ' A bird, madam,' offering a soggy, oiled guillemot. The bird was picked up far out at sea by a landing-craft, and the unavoidable delay before it could be brought in to me meant that there was little hope of recovery. Few of the birds arrive in such a ceremonial manner, but however they come, only a bird that is found soon after it struggles ashore and treated immediately has a prospect of recovery.

My first act is to wrap the poor creature in cotton-wool from bill to tail ; obviously, leaving the eyes and nostrils clear. It is then put into a wicker cat-basket which is closed and stood by the kitchen boiler ; and within this cocoon, warmth is soon generated and the damp feathers steam themselves dry, while some of the more liquid fuel oil is absorbed in the wool.

After a couple of hours the bird begins to perk up and now it can be unwrapped and fed. Persuading the new arrival to accept its first fish needs gentle persistence and takes perhaps an hour to achieve ; though the younger the bird, the sooner it will learn, because it is not so much a matter of learning as of remembering. From now until its release it must revert to a nestling frame of mind and look upon the human who provides food as a parent.

I believe that birds can think, up to a point, but most of their life is governed by patterns of behaviour suited to a given set of circumstances ; and after accepting food from my fingers a bird will automatically trust me because it would naturally only take a gift of food from a trusted parent or a mate during courtship.

A sense of taste is not generally presumed to be highly developed in birds, but I have found that a fulmar certainly knows the difference between raw haddock and other white fish, and will choose the haddock every time ; and so, with a new bird, if I can get it to taste the food I am offering, it will beg and feed voluntarily afterwards. Opening the bill of a shearwater, guillemot or petrel between forefinger and thumb, while inserting crosswise the second finger as a prop, is reasonably easy and allows small slivers of fish to be pushed in and tasted ; but the job becomes slightly more hazardous with a razorbill (which is well named), and a gannet is downright dangerous, as these birds can cut a hand to the bone with one slash of their formidable bills.

Gentleness and patience will soon tame a razorbill which, in common with all the auk family, is friendly by nature, but a gannet is very difficult to deal with at first and, for this reason, it is not easy to save them from pneumonia and the other secondary effects of pollution.

Those remarkable ladies, the Misses Yglesias, of the bird hospital at Mousehole, Cornwall, wrote to me after I had described my gannet problems on a B.B.C. television programme, suggesting that a thick woollen stocking pulled over the bird's head and lightly fastened round its neck would make it quite docile ; but I have not had an opportunity to try out this method. I have only played safe and shoved herrings, held in a pair of long brass coal-tongs, between the gannet's jaws whenever they snapped at me ; and the birds have been housed in an old-fashioned wicker laundry basket, bedded on dry straw and an old rug, with the lid firmly shut except at feeding-time.

The gannet is the largest British sea bird and has a wing-spread of six feet, is about three feet long and weighs up to eight pounds. The plumage of a young bird is brownish-black, speckled with white spots, but by the time it is four years old only the flight feathers remain black, while the rest of the body is pure white. I have described the bill as formidable and indeed it is ; like a road-mender's pick and very sharp, so that a herring caught sideways is sliced in two as if by a razor.

Gannets fish by soaring over the water until a shoal is sighted, when they descend in a power-dive from more than a hundred feet up, to plummet beneath the surface and hunt their prey. They often remain submerged for five seconds or more and are believed to go deep when necessary ; in fact, a number of them meet their end entangled in the trailing nets of trawlers. These birds are strictly denizens of the north Atlantic, and breed in the British Isles, Iceland and on the east coast of Canada, often forming vast colonies of several thousand pairs ; but as there is only one egg as a rule and the chick is abandoned to fend for itself when it is little more than two months old, the population remains more or less static.

A sea bird in temporary captivity is not easy to keep, and compared with a perching bird presents several problems. Their droppings are large, liquid and fishy ; and usually expelled with some force, because if the bird's hind-end is submerged in water while swimming, the excreta must be displaced against considerable pressure. When expelled on land it may travel several feet from larger birds like fulmars, with highly unpleasant consequences.

I am fortunate in having a back garden surrounded

by a wall, and so visiting birds can spend their days out of doors, either in pens or wandering free, where they are quite content in their own small areas, which are evidently looked upon as a territory or nest site.

Birds in an advanced stage of convalescence could spend the night out, too, if it were not for the army of prowling village cats which invades the garden after dark. The ideal alternative would be a conservatory but, failing this, my birds have to sleep in closed baskets by the kitchen window. They by no means resent this nightly incarceration and soon settle down in a nest of hay, picking up odd stems and arranging them with great care, although a guillemot or razorbill has no memory of a proper nest beyond the bare rock ledges on which these birds lay and brood their eggs.

The fishmonger's bill is another problem. Fish is eaten by most sea birds, except the smaller, plankton-eating species like storm-petrels and little auks, and these will probably take tinned sardine, prawn or shrimp meat mashed to a paste with cod-liver oil, whitebait, and perhaps morsels of cut herring. Sprats are the favourite diet of the larger birds, but unfortunately these are only in the shops for a limited season, and as an alternative one must use sprat-sized strips of herring.

Guillemots, razorbills, puffins, fulmars and other species of their weight (gulls are the same size or larger, but weigh less and eat less) will eat half a pound, or more, of fish every day ; in fact, on one occasion a guillemot took from my hand a dozen sprats in succession. Gannets can eat four or five herrings at a meal, and prove even more expensive guests.

One might expect sea-gulls to be some of the easiest species to handle, but this is far from being the case in practice, because of their instinctive habit of regurgitation, which makes them vomit the contents of the stomach when they are nervous. This is a protective habit designed to reduce the weight of the bird and increase its speed, and one which is battened upon by the skuas and great black-backed gulls who find part of their living by parasitising : forcing the gulls to disgorge a ready-made meal.

The gull is a very highly strung creature, and the more so when it is bereft of the power of flight, as it would be when kept in temporary captivity due to oiling or injury, and it knows the often cruel ways of man better than the pelagic, or ocean-going, birds. The result is that it is very difficult to manage and feed until it is tamed, and this may take several weeks. In the meantime, a thoughtless sudden movement on my part or a bark from one of the dogs will bring up all the food the bird has been persuaded to eat, and this is a great trial for one's patience.

Like sparrows, the commoner species of gulls have flourished in the footsteps of man, thriving and multiplying on the largess of garbage and fish offal offered by all the ports and coastal towns of the world. Indeed, the herring gull is fast becoming a pest, and steps are being taken to reduce its numbers where there are breeding colonies of rarer birds, as it is not above filching an unguarded egg or a chick or two from the nests of kittiwakes, guillemots and other cliff dwellers.

But though a garbage-eater in the wild, the domesticated gull quickly becomes a gourmet and refuses all but the best and freshest fish, perhaps condescending to take a little bread-and-milk now and then ; and one is only too glad to provide the best if it will stay down long enough to be digested.

One newly arrived patient, a herring gull still in the speckled plumage of youth, disgorged a small octopus, and that year I found another of these fascinating creatures stranded alive on the beach.

It is strange to be subjected to an intelligent scrutiny by this sad-eyed relative of the oyster, and I would have liked to attempt keeping it in an aquarium ; but the octopus is a notoriously difficult subject in captivity, and it was better returned to a pool left by the tide which would find it again in the evening. As I turned to go, a yard-wide area of the pool was being blackened by a smoke-screen of ink : a nervous gesture in line with the gull's regurgitant habit.

Food, apart from its cost and the patience needed to initiate a feeding-response from a new patient, is not a great problem ; but, oddly enough, water is often a serious worry, because an oiled bird that has narrowly escaped drowning in its once natural element develops a psychotic horror of it ; yet, without a daily intake of water its digestive system will break down, the kidneys will cease to function and the bird will gradually die. It is too easy to drown a bird by pouring water into its bill, and so other methods must be tried : the flesh of white fish will absorb a lot of water if it is soaked, and I rely on this a good deal while trying to persuade a nervous bird to drink voluntarily from a dish.

The white ' lime ' in a bird's droppings represent excretion from the kidneys, and in a healthy sea bird constitutes about seventy-five per cent of the total, so that with this as a guide it is quite possible to keep the bowels in correct working order, and give the bird a better chance of recovery.

Oceanic birds have no access to fresh water and must, therefore, drink from the sea, with a consequently high intake of salt which has to be eliminated. A large amount is dealt with by the kidneys and the remainder is secreted in fluid from a duct in the eye ; only a small proportion is retained for digestive purposes, and so it is not necessary to provide salt water for a sea bird to drink, as there is enough present in its diet of sea fish.

Reptiles living in salt or brackish water have the same processes for the disposal of salt, and this is shown particularly by a turtle which often appears to be weeping piteously.

All animal husbandry is a combination of common sense and knowledge, gained through research and practice ; and sea-bird management is no exception. The real problem is finding a method of cleaning

fuel oil from polluted plumage without causing
the further disorder ' wet-feather ', which is an almost
inevitable aftermath of oiling or injury, but varies in its
intensity according to the amount of rough treatment
the victim has endured.

There are two main causes of wet-feather : the
stress-induced failure of the oil-gland (a nipple-like
protuberance on the back above the tail, which provides lubrication and waterproofing for the plumage),
and a breakdown of the plumage itself as a warm
and buoyant body covering, which is largely caused
by the fumbling of inexpert and nervous hands. If
the disorder is due to the oil-gland alone, then the
bird may recover its buoyancy and waterproofing
quite soon, but if the feathering is affected, only a
complete moult will cure an attack of wet-feather.

Each feather in a bird's plumage is a highly
complicated piece of mechanism, designed to aid
flight and keep the bird warm, and to a varying
extent provide waterproofing.

The obvious structure shows a central shaft or quill
with a number of branches or barbs on each side ; the
whole presenting a solid elastic plane, unless it is
rubbed the wrong way, when the barbs will divide
into a row of hair-like bristles. Holding the feather
in a strong light it is possible to see that the barbs
are fringed at each side with barbules, which appear
as rows of tiny threads until suitably magnified, when
they show as a series of hooks that interlock one barb
to the next in much the same way as a zip-fastener,

producing the solid resiliency of a complete feather vane.

Pushing the barbs ' against the grain ' unlocks the barbules, but they are easily zipped again by stroking the feather towards its tip, and this is what a bird is doing when it preens, relinking the barbules that have come apart during the strain of flying or the disruption of bathing.

Naturally, on an active bird, the barbules are subject to a good deal of friction, and would soon fray if they were not oiled in the same way as cogs in a machine, and a preening bird greases each feather by taking beakfuls of oil from the uropygial gland at the base of its tail.

Experiments have shown that a barnyard cockerel deprived of this oil-gland quickly turned into a bedraggled wretch as his plumage dried and became brittle, allowing the barbules to unlock and break. This glandular secretion of oil has another purpose in providing weather-proofing. The land bird is soon soaked by rain and, knowing this, takes refuge when a shower begins ; but waterfowl are proof against all weather unless something is seriously wrong with their plumage. In their case the feathers are formed into a solid barrier by a waxy surface tension that actively repels water, and beneath this the skin is protected by a kind of pneumatic jacket produced by pockets of air trapped among the quills and down-feathers that lie under the visible plumage.

In normal circumstances it is impossible to imagine

a better arrangement than this warm, buoyant and almost weightless covering ; but if, owing to fuel-oil pollution or mishandling, the plumage of a sea bird is disrupted, then the whole mechanism breaks down and the bird is likely to drown unless it can get ashore quickly.

Equally, the failure of its oil-gland will render it helpless in its natural element ; and, if it is rescued, it will follow the same pattern as the experimental cockerel.

Oil-gland failure affected my first guillemot, and her progress illustrates the average pattern of recovery in such a case. Incidentally, the feminine gender is mere supposition, as it is impossible to tell the sexes apart, but ' she ' was so affectionate and fussy that one naturally looked on her as a female, and she was soon known as Gilly for short—as a rule I avoid naming a bird which is on a brief visit, as this seems rather ' twee ', but if you have a number of the same species in at one time, then it is, obviously, easier to tag them with names.

A terrible storm heralded Gilly's arrival : waves crashed over the sea-wall and in at our front gate, and workmen who were digging up the intervening road huddled round a coke stove as the wind and rain lashed over them. The tide turned and, glancing over the wall, one of the men saw a bedraggled object, rather like a miniature penguin, struggle out of the sea and collapse on the sand ; it was quite black with oil and soaked to the skin, and when they brought it to me it was shivering hard and I feared another pneumonia victim. But the cotton-wool treatment, a warm kitchen and slices of herring made a new bird by the evening, and though it was still very dirty it was possible to see the white markings on its head and breast as it sat up and began to preen.

Preening is a dangerous occupation for an oil-polluted bird, because although I do not believe that the oil is actively poisonous, it can block the respiratory and digestive systems with lethal consequences ; and so I decided to risk washing the guillemot at once.

By that time I had abandoned detergent in favour of pure soap-flakes as a cleaning agent, giving a warm bath in suds and two thorough rinses without using any grease beforehand ; which was a revolutionary step, but one could only experiment by trial and error.

After its bath and soaked to the skin once again, the bird was put in a nest of warm flannel in front of the dining-room gas fire, and it was here that I got a first glimpse of the charm that made Gilly one of my most extraordinary and best-loved birds, as she sat there enjoying the warmth that seeped through the damp feathers, taking time off to make a few idle threats at me with an open bill and then accepting a proffered piece of fish with evident satisfaction.

All my birds have to learn that dogs are harmless animals, except Gilly, who never minded them and quite soon learned that a recumbent Labrador made a comfortable perch.

After a week her plumage was clean and I could

see that she was an adult guillemot in winter colours :
the tail and back were black, narrowing to a black
line which followed the neck and then spread to cover
the head above the line of the eyes, while the rest of
the body from chin to tail was pure white, giving the
claw-hammer-suit effect of a penguin ; this is increased by the upright stance of these birds, so that
they appear to be sitting on the base of their tails,
with elbows (which are, in fact, the ankles) bent, and
webbed toes spread as the only counterbalance to
prevent them toppling forwards.

On land, guillemots are very unsteady on their
legs for more than short periods, and like to lean
against a pillow made of old rags or, better still, a
warm dog ; and so Gilly spent most of her time in
a low basket in the kitchen where she could watch
everything that went on and hop out with a whirr
of wings when she felt energetic.

In a month strength had returned sufficiently for
her to try a swim in a tidal pool, and from then on
she swam a little bit farther each day, though buoyancy
was only temporary and she had to scramble out before
beginning to sink. The set-up was exactly the same as
a nanny and a small child : I waited at the water's
edge with a towel, ready to wrap up the sopping bird
and carry it indoors to the fire and, as one might
expect, the daily dip always gathered an astonished
audience—or at least, grown-ups were bewildered ;
children have a wider horizon and see nothing odd
in the anthropomorphic behaviour of a wild sea bird,

and they are merely interested to watch its antics. And, as Gilly gained confidence, antics they were : she would dive and pop up like a cork ; race past under water, wings flapping and webbed feet paddling behind ; rear up above the surface and shake her wings and then dive again.

From a standing start she could travel under water at the rate of about two yards a second, but on the surface progress was much slower.

Three months after her arrival Gilly was buoyant for nearly half an hour at a time and I nerved myself to try her in the sea on a calm day, but I need not have worried ; she behaved exactly as she had always done : enjoyed her bathe and came ashore to the waiting towel, and so our circus act became even more popular with passers-by on the sands. The uninitiated would stare for a while until they could stand it no longer, and then they would tentatively inquire if the bird was a baby penguin, and I would reply with the nonchalance of a ring-master and throw in a lecture on oil pollution for good measure.

Gilly now went to sea every day whether the waves were high or not, evidently delighting in rough water and travelling out into the bay, so that at times she was only a speck of black in the distance ; but I had enough confidence to leave her and watch from the windows of the house until she came ashore.

It seemed remarkable that she should know exactly where to arrive, until one remembered that a nesting guillemot must find its solitary egg on a featureless cliff-face in the midst of perhaps a thousand egg-laden ledges, every time it comes back from a fishing expedition.

The future seemed bright, and every day I expected the bird to go off into the Atlantic following the call of her nature ; yet always there she was on the sands waiting to be brought into the fire and her supper ; until one evening she did not come and I thought she had gone—before I saw a small object huddled on the tide-line in the light of the setting sun. She had come up against another of the secondary effects of pollution, heart disease, and within three days she was dead.

Since then I have carried out a post-mortem examination of every dead patient, and in all cases have found evidence of a burst aneurysm as the cause of death, unless pneumonia was the killer. I conclude that the oiled bird's struggle shorewards puts too great a strain on its heart, and if it does not die then, a weakness often remains.

Gilly's wild games in the sea were too violent for a convalescent bird, and finally her heart just puttered to a stop, for she died peacefully while I gently scratched the back of her head.

I had learned another lesson about the care of sea birds, and knew then that any form of exertion must be approached by degrees, and fatigue prevented at all costs.

The next bird patient must be a very rare example. It was a racing-pigeon, which came down in a state of exhaustion and took refuge in a garage, where it landed in a pool of sump oil. When it arrived for treatment, the poor bird was a solid mass of glutinous black oil, the feathers glued together in lumps. I washed it in soap suds, after buttering the worst patches, and then powdered the plumage with pre-pared chalk. The next morning the powder was rinsed out in tepid water, and after three days' rest the pigeon flew off on the remainder of its journey, none the worse for the experience.

This quick and successful treatment serves to pin-point the essential difference between caring for a wild sea bird and a domesticated species, accustomed to being handled and without an urgent need for waterproof plumage.

After that I experimented with prepared chalk as a sort of dry shampoo, and used this on several razor-bills. With this method the bird is powdered on arrival and then given the usual cotton-wool treat-ment. The action is much slower, but it does mean that the bird can be kept warm and dry from the first, as rinsing out the powder may be delayed for several days until the bird has gained strength. How-ever, the method is far from ideal, because alkali substances are bad for feathers ; but as some ninety-five per cent of all oiled birds are subject to wet-feather anyway, this is not a very serious consideration until a cure for the disorder is found. A correspondent had tried the alkali-free detergent Stergene on an individual guillemot, which was successful from the cleansing point of view but left the bird with the usual blotting-paper plumage.

Clearly, wet-feather itself is not lethal and, if the bird can be kept alive in the interim, it will wear off. The causes of death are those that I have already described : pneumonia, deterioration of the kidneys and heart disease.

One more remains, and this came to light during dissection. A high percentage of waterfowl carry internal parasites, from coccidiosis to intestinal worms, and in normal circumstances suffer no harm ; but in a state of physical weakness the parasites appear to establish a firmer hold and can become so numerous that the host finally dies.

In addition, it seems to me very possible that pathological study might show that hitherto unexplained deaths due to degeneration of an internal organ could be the result of over-secretion by the adrenal gland, following the fear and exhaustion caused by the bird's struggle shorewards after oiling or injury. Certainly, adrenalin has been proved to have a dire effect on laboratory rats subjected to great effort or stress.

Meanwhile, with the odds apparently insuperable, one might be entitled to throw in the sponge, but even a few survivors to be returned to the wild make continued work worth while ; and, of course, the failures provide knowledge that will mean one mistake less in the future.

CHAPTER THREE : A QUEST FOR CORVIDS

THE crow tribe as a whole, and magpies in particular, have a bad name. This seems a pity to me.
I doubt whether they do more harm to fledglings than,
say, kestrels or other birds of prey ; and from my
observations of tame magpies they appear to destroy
a number of pests and are not keen on eggs as anything but a small addition to their diet.

I have reared two magpies. The first, Tom, lived
long enough to endear himself to my heart, and then
was killed by a stray dog. Piper came the following
spring. He was found in the back-yard shed of a
terrace house in the centre of a neighbouring town,
perched dismally on the handle-bars of a parked
bicycle, dishevelled and starving. How he came there
is still a mystery, and it was only luck that brought
him to light before two cats arrived to take up their
lawful sleeping-quarters for the night.

Like all young corvids, Piper soon learned to trust
his own humans and enjoy the role of pet ; showing
the family traits of affection, mischief and humour,
and a love of possessions. It saddens me to see
ravens, jackdaws and magpies kept in the clinically
tidy cages of a zoo, their normally active brains
atrophied with boredom ; a happy crow is a busy
one, employed in searching crannies for insects,

investigating the contents of a match-box or tearing something to shreds and hiding the pieces in a special cache. These secret stores can be numerous, and a free-flying magpie remembers them all, becoming very cross if one finds a pile of these precious possessions during cleaning operations.

Piper would chatter with rage if I watched him tuck a bit of biscuit behind a picture frame and then removed it when he had done ; yet he often proffered gifts to me. He gave me food with great ceremony, chirruping with a noise like a strangled hiccup and making a courtship display with fluttered wings and quick flips of his long tail. Other presents such as silver-paper were more often hidden in my pockets and the cuff of a jersey, and these were only on loan, for if I touched them they were snatched back and gulped into his chin-pouch, while he scolded in a high-pitched series of squawks.

My typewriter has always been a source of fascination to the crows. It has provided an ideal ground in which to hide food, beer-bottle caps, cigarette ends and a dozen other valuable objects ; but at the same time it is a dangerous thing concealing a red-and-black snake. Piper was happily pulling out yards of ribbon when he suddenly recognised its serpentine shape and leapt to safety on the back of my chair, where he perched on tiptoe and made a peculiar, shrill, trilling sound which is only given as the alarm for extreme danger.

I heard this cry from him several times, usually

because he could see something that, with a stretch of the imagination, might appear to be a snake ; but once he did it at the sight of one of his own flight feathers which he had moulted out on to the aviary floor ; and again for a woman in a red hat.

One of the oddest facets of the crow mind is the universal fear of black, which is at the same time the dominant colour in all their plumage, except in the case of the jay.

Perhaps their eyesight picks out the refracted blues and greens of healthy crow feathers and looks upon matt black as a dead colour to inspire horror. Certainly, gardeners could take advantage of this fear and beg used typewriter ribbons from local offices to festoon over the peas and fruit, which no amount of cat's-eyes or tangled cotton threads can protect.

Next to black, red is also feared or, rather, disliked. An old cock jackdaw became attached to a red-painted cage and considered it his territory, defending it against Piper, who thought it fun to play 'last across' by dashing in and out of the open door with his head bowed to avoid the enraged pecks of its owner ; but that was only contempt bred of familiarity, and on the whole most birds avoid red.

Blue is the favourite colour of every species I have known. At one time I kept a collection of canaries, budgerigars, and small African finches at liberty in a conservatory where each pair had its own cage in which to eat and roost. Most of the cages were large and of the box type used for breeding budge-rigars, but one was a small and rather rusty all-wire affair with nothing to recommend it beyond the vital fact that it was painted blue. This blueness made it the dream home of every bird, and each night found them packed into it like sardines in a tin.

Piper had a blue cage in which to roost, and he was released from this every morning for a pre-breakfast tour of the village before returning to spend the day in an outdoor aviary. Adjoining this was the cage housing my old jackdaw whose flying days were over. Gunshot wounds had broken a wing and lamed his right leg, and I suppose he ought to have been destroyed ; but I am loath to kill a bird unless it is obviously in pain and maimed beyond any possibility of recovery, because I have seen so many apparently hopeless cases recover and gain vigour to return to the wild successfully.

The jackdaw failed to reach this standard, but he established himself as one of the family and found a friend in Piper. The two had a curious daily reunion in the form of a mock fight through the intervening wire. At intervals each pretended submission, the jackdaw by bowing and offering the nape of his neck, while Piper, after the manner of his species, did the opposite : standing rigid and tall with the bill point-ing upwards like a bittern, presumably offering his throat. The party went on for a while and then ended in an exchange of gifts—paper, cardboard boxes and so forth—which were provided to keep them happily employed during the day. Their chatter was only silenced during the hour surrounding natural midday, when the sun is at its zenith and all birds settle for a rest.

Magpies are omnivorous and will eat anything remotely edible. In captivity the staple diet is poultry meal, porridge oats, bread-and-milk, raw and cooked meat, fruit and nuts.

Oddly enough, fish is very popular, as I discovered when Piper showed an intense interest in the garden pond and one day succeeded in landing a large, and much prized, shubunkin goldfish—which I was fortunately able to retrieve undamaged. From his expert approach to the sport, it seems evident that wild magpies must often catch fish in shallow ponds and streams. Piper took this addiction further and would snatch sardines and raw herrings or cod intended for my sea birds.

Deciding just what a feeding magpie was actually eating might be a difficult job for an observer in the field, because these birds tend to pick up and deposit in their chin-pouches anything that catches their eyes. They will take beetles and other fast-moving creatures for the mere interest of dismembering the unfortunate victim, but on the other hand pounce like cats on unwary mice and eat them with evident relish.

When I switched on the light one night it illuminated a mouse in the act of eating Piper's supper ; I kept still to see what would happen, and was astonished at the rapidity with which the bird woke up, saw his prey and jumped. His bill thumped the cage floor like a knife-thrower's dagger, but the mouse had dodged between the dish and the wall and lay hidden. Then Piper and I settled down to wait, both of us quite unmoving and silent, until the reassured mouse peered out from its refuge. Instantly it was transfixed by the jabbing bill and shaken to death like a rat in the jaws of a terrier. Nothing but the skin and a few bits remained in the morning.

A rat, however, was a different matter. Piper observed one from a safe perch on the hen-house roof, looking down on the foraging animal with his head cocked but obviously preferring the better part of valour.

I was watching it, too, and wishing a ·410 were handy; but on another day I stood contemplating the offspring of that rat as they tottered from a hole in the hedge, blinked at the sunlight and then began to try their new legs, young country rats with black guard-hairs adding even more lustre to their glossy brown fur, unsure of themselves at first and then gaining confidence and scampering together in mock battle and chase-me-Charlie round the currant bushes. Young candidates for steel traps and red squill poison, they shared a misfortune in common with the crows and some of my other birds : human economics made them vermin.

In Devon they used to put corn rats in the vats of scrumpy cider ; rat cider had more body to it, they said. Piper never had the chance to try cider, rat or otherwise, but he had a great taste for gin—and a shockingly weak head. When we were left with the squalor that is the inevitable aftermath of a cocktail party, he would skip from one glass of dregs to another, taking a sip from each and becoming more vociferous and unbalanced every minute. Birds live at a fast rate, and he took the sensations of an alcoholic in quick succession, from polite sipping and small talk, through singing and watch-me-balance-on-this . . . whoops ! . . . and ending in glum silence, perched on one leg, head tucked under fluffed-up mantle ; the whole gamut run within half an hour.

A lot of birds will take to drink, given the opportunity ; ducks like beer, and ravens at the Tower of London sometimes invade the officers' mess to drink port after dinner, and at least one individual has subsequently fallen out of the window to its death on the flagstones below, drunk and incapable. But funny as the antics of a drunk bird may be, I would not allow mine more than a very rare chance at the bottle—unless they were ill.

Whisky or brandy is often given to a sick bird in the belief that this will revive it, but usually does more harm than good. Gin, on the other hand, is an excellent pick-me-up for ailing birds, which may be due to some medicinal property in juniper berries.

The partnership lasted quite a long time, but in the end Piper's interest in the fish pond caused the death of the old jackdaw. On nice days the two were allowed out to mess about in the garden together, and on the last occasion I had looked to see if they were contented and then spent twenty minutes writing a letter before again going out, to find a sodden black object floating on the surface of the pond, drowned beyond recall.

Sometimes it is possible to save a drowned bird by holding it upside down by the legs so that the water can run out of the windpipe, but this treatment had no effect on an utterly dead jackdaw.

Soon afterwards a mournful Piper left me, too ; I hope and believe that he joined a small flock of his kind which lives in a wood beyond the village.

But I was not bereft of corvids for long. The first was a fledgling jackdaw, found sitting in innocent defiance amongst a slavering company of farm cats. He was young enough to fear nothing, and was soon strongly attached to his human family and to the dogs ; and insatiable in his demands for pellets of poultry meal and milk which had to be thrust down his gaping throat with a forefinger.

Within a week or so he had learned to feed himself and to fly, and in a short time he was touring the village and hoarding a nice collection of hard cash, safety-pins and unguarded jewellery. Then one night he was not home at dusk, and the next morning he was still missing, and after that he was never seen again. A pair of nesting barn owls were suspect (the ground beneath their tree was littered with young jackdaws' legs), and that was the end of his story ; but a paragraph in the local newspaper, describing a tame jackdaw found in a garden some miles away, prompted a letter asking for news of my own lost bird. This was an error. Within twenty-four hours I had become the owner of a tame jackdaw (not the missing one), and a fledgling raven. The last arrived on the pillion of a motor bicycle with a triumphant youth who said : ' I've got something here that belongs to you,' handing me this monstrous and disreputable fledgling. It perched heavily on my hand, inspected me with a large brown eye and said something guttural in Low Dutch.

From then on, apart from the hours of darkness, its conversation was ceaseless and incomprehensible, punctuated occasionally with bouts of Chaliapin-like singing and hoarse shouts for food.

Given a nice literary name, Barnaby thrived and gradually shed his grubby brown feathers for a coat of shining blue-black ; his bill stopped gaping like a pink-lined Gladstone bag and he learned to pick up and swallow chunks of meat and bread-and-milk and take a daily bath.

Crows attach great importance to baths, and from fledgling-hood onwards like to get really soaked at least once a day.

When adult birds moult through their new winter plumage, the feathers are so strongly water-repellent that however much the frustrated owner may dip and flutter in its bath, the water streams off as if it were wearing an oilskin mackintosh ; but young birds have no such proofing and also lack the adult's undercoat

of down-feathers. Because of this, the newly bathed
fledgling appears ludicrous and almost stark naked in
its scant and sopping plumage, and one is inclined to
worry about pneumonia, but this instinctive cleanli-
ness has a purpose. When the feather buds break
through a young bird's skin and the growing quill
casts off its encasing shell, a litter of scurf-like debris
remains as an ideal breeding-ground for grey lice and
a horrid kind of parasitic flightless fly, *Crataerina* ;
both of which die fairly rapidly when immersed in
water. The fly attached to the *Corvidae* is brown in
colour, but this evidently is not an attempt at camou-
flage, because the dark-brown swift carries an apple-
green variety of the same fly.

Cleanly—and who is to say, not godly?—the metamorphosis was almost imperceptible, yet day by day
Barnaby became more beautiful and imposing. There
was no doubt of his predatory nature : large forward-
set eyes above a four-inch bill shaped like an ice-pick,
and feet tipped with sharp claws. Savagely he
attacked a sheep's head intended for the dogs' dinner,
and yet equally beneath this stark exterior he was the
most sentimental of birds and the most highly strung.
New shapes and odd shadows conjured up all sorts of
horrors in his brain, which appeared to be completely
demoralised by unfounded fears, making him hurtle
about the room uttering harsh croaks of distress.
Experience taught me how to avoid most of these
frights, but they still happened now and again, often
leaving the poor fellow voiceless for half a day.

While the new tame jackdaw, who became known as Orry, loved all humans, though principally attached to my mother, Barnaby was selective. He would talk to the family and allow himself to be stroked by them, but strangers were ignored. With me he was over-demonstrative, perching on my head and shoulders, pilfering my pockets and forever conversing in idle chat.

All corvids have a chin-pouch for storing food and other items which are not immediately swallowed. With the rook, the baldness of the area round its bill makes the pouch more obvious, but the other species can look like pelicans on occasions, though the distended skin is hidden by a covering of small feathers.

As a highly comical joke, Barnaby often tried to decant his pouch down the back of one's neck: a nice mixture of bread, milk, meat and a particularly glutinous saliva. His digestive system seemed to be much the same as that of real birds of prey, and in the morning the tray under his perch was often littered with pellets—neat parcels containing indigestible oddments of string, paper, match-sticks and the like, which had been regurgitated during the night.

This faculty must frequently have been the saving of him, for he was always snatching and bolting the most unsuitable objects, from cigarette ends to rubber bands.

While sentimental to a degree, perched almost in a state of catalepsy while his head and back were being stroked, or rubbing his face against one's ear,

Barnaby was just as mischievous as the rest of the crow family. It was principally the dogs who suffered from his attentions, for teasing was his special line, and dogs' tails were there to be tweaked. He would even try to take their bones, but this was not allowed, as there are limits to the best dog's endurance.

Teasing aside, he was evidently fond of the Labradors and the beagle, and often perched near them when all were settled for an afternoon snooze. Curiosity led him to join in imaginary mouse-hunts, and produced the surely unique sight of the beagle peering under the end of a bureau while Barnaby, crouched on his elbows beside her, stared too, in the ardent hope of seeing whatever it was that she saw.

A raven about the house tended to lower our standard of living quite considerably as time went on, and banishment to a large indoor cage and the freedom of the garden was the only answer ; but, fortunately, Barnaby was content for hours on end if his cage contained articles for him to tear up, and he was convinced that these were valuable and badly needed by me.

His outings were more of a problem because he was far from intrepid and flew wildly about the housetops trying to pluck up enough courage to pancake on someone's television aerial, and in this manner used to travel farther than he meant to and get lost.

On these occasions Orry, the jackdaw, who normally ignored the raven as nothing more than a noisy great nuisance, would go into action and retrieve his panic-struck relative. His tactics were to gain verbal contact with the lost one by a series of caws which Barnaby answered, *basso profundo*, from afar. Orry then flew directly to him and proceeded to make a step-by-step return, flying always some fifty feet ahead and calling all the time. When the prodigal finally made a landfall on our back garden and came panting into the kitchen, the jackdaw would make off on his own affairs.

One must not be trapped into giving a bird anthropomorphic motives ; tradition or instinct or what-have-you makes all sorts of birds react to a fledgling in distress, and in this case the fact that Barnaby was part of Orry's ' family ' was an added incentive.

With the arrival of another spring, I was faced with the problem of a mate for Barnaby. As with so many species, the difficulty was increased by a lack of any guide to a raven's sex ; only the birds themselves know what they are, and often they need to go through an elaborate mutual display before they can be sure of the sex of another individual of their kind. This sort of display is commonly seen in robins, and more magnificently in the great crested grebe.

However, Barnaby solved the problem for me. By then, he was flying independently and farther each day, and in the end he went feral altogether.

About three months later we met again when I was walking with the dogs over some scrub land a mile or so from home ; above us the familiar ' *cruck, crruck* ' sounded and a vast black bird swooped low, almost brushing my head. Then another raven called, and Barnaby answered as he flew ponderously on his way.

CHAPTER FOUR : ORRY AND OTHERS

ORRY lived with us for nearly three years, and all but the first few months of that time he spent at liberty ; free to come and go as he pleased, and to find a wild mate and raise a family.

As he was brought in on the same day that Barnaby came, and I was busy enough trying to meet the insatiable demands of the young raven, he became particularly attached to my mother, who had undertaken the job of rearing him. In the early days he was just another fledgling jackdaw, squawking and gaping for dollops of bread-and-milk ; but soon we became aware that Orry was different.

In common with a surprising number of other species, jackdaws have a strong homing instinct, and so it is an easy matter to keep them in the same way as pigeons, when they quickly learn the local terrain and to enter the house by an open window or door.

It was wonderful to watch Orry negotiate the stairs in flight. They are two-thirds enclosed and in the form of a leg, with a small landing half-way up, and steep into the bargain. This meant that from upstairs the bird had to fly downwards at an angle to four o'clock, straighten out and turn sharp right before continuing down. He did it at full speed, ending in a swoop that took him into the kitchen, where his dishes of food and water were kept ready on a shelf.

After a snack he then demanded a bath, and this was provided in an old blue-patterned soup tureen normally used as the dogs' drinking-bowl. Orry stamped about on the draining-board while his bath was filled, and then hopped on to the rim to try the water with first one foot and then the other, rather like those unhappy people who bathe in the Serpentine at Christmas. Finally, his mind made up, he took the plunge. Bathing for Orry was an athletic business which rose in crescendo until most of the kitchen floor was awash. The performance began with a few tentative swizzles with the bill to wet his head and chest, before the serious part, which involved squatting with spread tail and fluttering wings to send a sheet of water forwards over his back and, incidentally, fountaining out of the bowl.

After about five minutes he struggled out, soaking wet and so heavy with water that he was unable to raise his weight off the ground with sodden wings, and so it was the duty of whoever was around at the time to offer a hand for him to climb on to, and then carry him across to the dresser, where he perched like an omen of doom until his plumage was dry enough to preen.

Bathed and fed, his next engagement was with the holiday-makers on the sands. During high summer the road beside the sea-wall is lined with parked cars, and these were well worth a visit. Tame birds seem to go to peoples' heads more than any other kind of animal, and when Orry arrived on a car bonnet and began dismantling the windscreen-wiper, an enchanted audience would surround him, offering titbits from picnic baskets, chocolate and ice-cream, and, most foolishly, money. People who have not met a crow before seldom realise how quickly it can snatch a small object and depart to some chimney-stack where the prize will be lost forever. I was going in at our gate one day when I noticed a woman shaking her fist in the direction of the roof, and glanced up to see Orry earnestly poking something down one of the chimneys. The something was a child's sock which turned up on the sitting-room hearth several days later.

Children had his special love, and most of them reciprocated it, though a few were unnerved at having their toes nipped. Mostly they had the same ideas as he did : building sand-castles from which he could remove the decorative shells and paper flags and then play tag with the trophy, always one hop out of reach.

Such a Disney character could hardly fail to attract, and any evening when he was late home we were afraid that someone had taken the chance of stealing him. But he was still there when the winter came : a very bored bird without the cars and admiring crowds, and consequently a menace in the home. The interior of a house and its furnishings offer plenty of scope, and I learned the hard way to keep all the things normal people have on their dressing-tables in a drawer ; and to abandon thoughts of pot plants and vases of flowers. The kitchen was under siege, too. Here anything in a paper bag was fair game and, all in all, one was relieved when Orry took the day off, unless he stayed away too long, when we began to worry and search.

To a magpie, flying is nothing more than a means of getting from here to there, but jackdaws enjoy and perfect it as an art with as much zest as a human gliding enthusiast. As Orry grew up, his flying technique increased, and by mid-winter he was hurtling past the upstairs windows doing his version of the victory-roll, swooping and towering, and cawing his triumph in this mastery of the air.

In the course of one power-dive he removed, in passing, the hair-net of an irate lady who had been lost in contemplation of the view from the sea-wall.

With the arrival of spring and the beginning of warm sunshine he began to show symptoms of sunning-display. This behaviour is shown by many species, but more markedly by those in which a dark colour predominates. All the crow tribe react to the sun, and so do blackbirds and starlings. The cause is a subject of controversy.

The effect is that a bird busy about its affairs enters a shaft of sunlight which is hotter than the half-shade it was in a second or two ago ; and then, though its thoughts are evidently still intent, the body appears to respond independently. The bird stops in its tracks, fans its tail and with outspread wings subsides to the ground, where it lies as if cataleptic, with one eye cocked towards the sun.

This display may last only half a minute or so, but it can go on for quite a long time, during which the bird is more or less rigid like a pointer dog winding a grouse, and yet gives the impression that the sensation is intensely satisfying.

Sunning-display behaviour should not be confused with the lackadaisical attitudes of farmyard hens or dust-bathing sparrows. The real display has a definite pattern and is, I am certain, involuntary. As I have said, the subject is a controversial one, and so much so that I argue between my own theories.

One relates colour and heat absorption to the normal body temperature. The metabolic rate of birds is very high indeed ; for instance, the house-sparrow breathes ninety times each minute, while its heart beats eight hundred times, and its body maintains an average temperature of 107° F. The crow tribe have the same temperature as a sparrow, but other species which display in the sun, such as blackbirds, thrushes and starlings, can vary between 111·2 and 113° F.

From the point of view of sunning-display, a blackbird and a crow can be compared in spite of the difference in their size because, although one is very much smaller, it offers a relatively larger external surface which requires a higher body temperature to preserve it in a temperate climate, and also makes it supersensitive to external changes in temperature.

As dark pigments absorb heat to a greater extent than pale colours, this suggests that birds like black-birds and crows, possessing black plumage, might suffer a marked rise in temperature in strong sun-light. When the bird is perched or on the ground, its body is compact, enfolded by the largest feathers of the wings, which again tend to incapsulate the absorbed heat. When this heat reached a given point above normal, a physical reaction would be expected to occur, as it does in man and horses in the form of secretion from the sweat-glands. It seems likely that sunning-displays have the same cause, and that spreading the wings and tail in a particular manner increases the bird's body area and reduces its heat. That is one explanation ; another is more fundamental. One of the odd things about the study of natural history is that few ornithologists are interested in herpetology ; yet reptiles are close relatives of the birds and share many features in common. The most obvious one is their response to sunshine.

I have kept the British viviparous lizard for observation and found that its behaviour was start-lingly similar to that of birds from the point of view of basking or sunning. An adult male became very tame and liked to bask on the palm of my hand, the two sides of his belly flattened and extended to catch the warmth, and his head cocked in the direction of the sun or the radiance of a fire. At first he felt cold against my skin; then he acquired my temperature and became barely discernible, and from that stage took up a positive heat of his own, generated by the sun's rays.

His attitude was as nearly identical with that of a sunning bird as it is possible for a wingless creature to achieve, and this might suggest that sunning-displays by birds are promoted by inheritance from cold-blooded forebears of the primeval forests.

These hypotheses, however, are nothing but guesses based on more or less casual observations. In the realm of fact, there is a clear pointer towards a true reason for the display. In the wild, birds seldom perform the cataleptic display, whereas the same species kept in captivity will sun themselves regularly. A correspondent, who shared my interest in this phenomenon, toured the aviaries of a large zoo on an unusually hot day, noting the species responding to the sun, and his findings showed that the majority were birds with dark plumage—ranging from a condor to a hornbill.

On the other hand, I watched wild jackdaws and rooks which habitually perched on a warehouse roof in a nearby town, and although the slates must have been blisteringly hot on a sunny day, the birds were never observed to do anything but perch in a normal manner. It must, therefore, be concluded that captivity has some special effect, and this would be explained by the discovery made by a Chinese physiologist, Hsiang-chuan Hou, some thirty years ago. He showed that preen-oil secreted by the uropygial gland contains ergosterol, which changes into Vitamin D when the oil has been spread on a bird's plumage and exposed to irradiation by sunlight. This explains the two distinct kinds of preening employed by all birds ; in the first instance, oil is taken from the gland in beakfuls and attached to the feathers ; then, after a suitable interval, the bird preens again ; this time without resorting to the gland but, instead, taking minute globules of vitamin-fortified oil from the sun-warmed plumage and swallowing it.

Clearly, a bird in captivity, or even one like Orry who, although he was free, chose to spend a lot of the day indoors, would get less vitamin-producing sunlight than its wild counterpart, and might well react instinctively with a display that suffused its plumage to the greatest extent when the opportunity occurred. A wild bird would behave in a similar manner after a prolonged spell of bad weather, and in both cases the behaviour is in line with that of mammals suffering from diet deficiencies, who will eat filth, earth and even stones in an instinctive attempt to find the missing vitamins or minerals.

Orry flourished in his chosen way of life, and by April, when he was almost twelve months old, he was in full adult plumage and a very smart bird : small by crow standards, measuring about thirteen inches in length and weighing half a pound. His plumage was jet black, refracted by the sun into glinting blues and mauves, with a patch of light grey which extended down the back of his neck and over the ears. His legs and feet were black.

In most species of birds, the legs are scaly and rather reptilian, but the crows appear to be wearing somewhat clumsily wound patent-leather puttees. Orry's legs were polished to match his plumage, and he looked very dapper as he strode about the garden with the characteristic prancing walk of the jackdaw. It was not long before he attracted members of a flock of his kind, and one hen in particular.

As a general rule, jackdaws mate in their second season, but he had been early hatched and fed like a fighting-cock throughout his domesticated life, and so was prepared to breed sooner than usual.

Turmoil ensued, because the nest was the only thing that mattered, and Orry would burst into the house demanding building-materials, flying round the kitchen and snatching anything we could find to offer him—bits of cloth, cotton-wool, paper, string and cardboard, sticks and straws—until his bill was full. Then, getting his load airborne with difficulty, he flew off, trailing streamers behind him, only to return a few minutes later with renewed demands. This nest must have been a magnificent structure, but I never saw it as the site was high in the chimney of the local pub.

At last the nest was finished and we had peace for

about two weeks while his mate brooded the eggs ; but once they were hatched, work was continuous from dawn to dusk. Orry arrived at regular intervals to fill his chin-pouch from a constant supply of food, except for the one or two occasions when we forgot to refill the dish and were hunted out by the enraged bird, who landed on a shoulder, hissing and snapping his bill with fury.

The young were in the nest for just over a month, and by the end of that time the endless journeying had taken its toll of Orry's strength. Quite often he was unable to raise himself from the dish to the top of the sash-window, and had to be lifted up so that he had enough height for take-off. But when the fledglings were out, he brought them to a pergola near the kitchen window and fed them there.

Only two survived : a Mutt and Jeff pair, one tall and thin and the other squat and round. The mate appeared only rarely, and then just to scold Orry from a distance for his apparently lunatic attachment to a houseful of dangerous humans.

In due course the young jackdaws became self-supporting, and some time after that their mother must have been killed, because by the end of the summer Orry was a house bird once more. He slept in an attic room which was set aside for him, and spent the day messing about the house and garden, or riding on my mother's shoulder wherever she went. Bed-making amused him particularly, and he loved burrowing under the top sheet and running about like a surfacing mole while she tried to shoo him out and put on the blankets.

The bathroom was fascinating, too, and he would skitter along the edge of the bath, just saving himself from slipping in with whoever was trying to have a bath at the time.

Nothing frightened Orry, with the exception of loud bangs. A slammed door or a car back-firing sent him hurtling to my mother for protection; which was a very unusual reaction for a basically wild bird who was not imprinted to her in the sense of ignoring his kind in her favour.

Birds become imprinted to human beings or other creatures all too easily, and for their own sakes it is important to try and prevent the occurrence of this mental state, which, if it is allowed to take hold, will spoil their lives.

A fulmar became imprinted to me, refusing food, and spitting at anyone who tried to care for it in my absence. This was a hopeless situation, and I had to destroy the bird for that reason: a sad decision, as the fulmar was full of character and apparently content with the prospect of spending a lifetime in a garden enclosure, provided that I was always in attendance.

Beyond a wish to be with us, Orry never showed active devotion and was, in fact, very rough and inclined to bite bare toes or twist the lobe of an ear with savage enjoyment: quite unlike the magpies, who are incredibly gentle, or Barnaby, who was almost too sentimental and yet went wild very easily.

As each corvid is an original personality, it is difficult to compare the I.Q.s of my various species, but Orry was probably the most intelligent. Certainly he exhibited both a capacity for thought and, on one occasion at least, a rather macabre sense of humour.

At that time I had a hen blackbird convalescing from serious injuries, and she was at the stage where it was necessary to re-educate her taste for natural foods before she was released. So, a daily job was to dig up a dozen earthworms, and my mother was doing this for me, watched by Orry. After a while he flew off and returned carrying a large and lively worm, landed on her shoulder and, despite every protest, pushed it firmly down the collar of her dress. Cries of distress brought me to the scene and, if it were possible, I should have said that Orry wore a grin.

A jackdaw's bill is not made for digging, and they do not eat worms, which seems to prove a humorous motive—though perhaps it was triggered in the first instance by an instinctive desire to offer food to a loved one.

Time was running out for Orry. He spent the next spring as a solitary widower, strongly resenting the arrival of a fledgling jackdaw which I reared but had to keep separate for fear of Orry's murderous intentions. The summer came, and with it a large crop of green peas in a neighbour's garden.

Jackdaws are, undoubtedly, destructive birds and can damage vegetables and other crops, but they are also very nervous creatures, and it is quite possible to keep them in check by hanging up black cloths or by impaling red-painted bottles on stakes, besides using nets.

Orry, with his trust of all humanity, had the fatal misfortune to meet a gardener who preferred to use a gun. He was evidently hit by the shot when he was flying fairly high, because I found his body by the road. And so a friendship that had lasted since he was six weeks old ended.

The death of Orry made me resolve to refuse a home to any other corvids, and to encourage the remaining one to go feral at the earliest possible moment. While I lived in the centre of a village, it no longer seemed right to gain the confidence of birds who might ultimately lose their lives through a misplaced trust of human beings. I kept this resolution for more than a year, and then it was broken by force of circumstances.

I came in one Sunday evening and found a cardboard box in the hall, with a note attached saying that it contained a blackbird which had been taken from a cat. True enough, the bird inside was black, but it was a fledgling jackdaw, uninjured and gaping hungrily. A few days later another arrived, and shortly after that Phillip came, again in a cardboard box and incognito. His rescuer said, ' I don't know what it is but it's rather large ! ' He was indeed large : a carrion crow about two months old, and showing symptoms of what appeared to be incipient pneumonia. And so there I was, once more stuffing food down eager throats.

For more than a week I was involved in other work, and could find time only to feed the birds and keep them clean and, as a result, Phillip saw more of the dogs than he did of me, and attached himself to them with extraordinary devotion. At that age a young crow is fairly inactive and spends most of its time perched in a semi-comatose condition until the next meal arrives. Phillip was even quieter, as he was far from well, though a nightcap of three drops of gin in a spoonful of milk each evening had smoothed his ruffled feathers and brought him back to life, so that after the first week he began to put on weight.

His diet was fifty per cent carnivorous, consisting of bread-and-milk plus an equal amount of raw and cooked meat and fat, and one halibut-oil capsule a day. These capsules are easy to administer and are very effective for larger land and sea birds, but too concentrated for a bird smaller than a pigeon.

When I had time to spare for the birds again, I found that the dogs were the rather embarrassed and morose owners of a pet carrion crow, who followed them about either on foot or perched on their backs, and slept in one or other of their beds. The two Labradors shared a bed, and often sandwiched the beagle between them ; now they sandwiched the crow, too. However, as I was the provider of food,

I was able partially to detach him from this one-track and one-sided love in favour of the advantage of riding on my shoulder and perching on the back of the chair while I wrote. Oddly enough, he would defend this vantage-point against the dogs, threatening them with an open bill.

Like Barnaby, he was very highly strung and subject to hysterical fright, and yet he enjoyed making a bed as much as Orry did, and a symphony concert on the radio was always accompanied by loud, off-key gargles and caws, which culminated in a bout of coughing.

I still believed that this cough was bronchial in origin, as the weather had been bad during the week-end when he was found, and a hungry bird is very subject to chills.

A closer acquaintance had brought to light the fact that Phillip was crawling with grey lice, and I decided to allow him a bath on a hot day, so that debris and eggs from these creatures could be cleaned up. The lice themselves were quickly eradicated with pyrethrum powder, which, unlike DDT and other chlorinated hydrocarbon insecticides, is completely harmless to birds.

As one might expect of a corvid, his first bath was a very thorough affair that left him partially naked on the throat and breast, until the feathers dried and were preened back into place ; and it was while he was in this condition that I saw the cause of his cough : a hole the size of a farthing just above the

' wish-bone ', probably made by a slug from an airgun or ·22 rifle.

It may seem odd that I had not discovered this wound before, but my policy is to avoid handling wild birds as much as possible, because they dislike it intensely. The new arrival is given a superficial inspection for obvious injuries, like fractures, which would need attention, but anything else is best left for nature to heal. In Phillip's case nature was already doing a good job, gathering together the edges of the wound as if by a draw-string and covering it with a healthy scab. The cough was probably due to the formation of scar tissue near his windpipe.

The carrion crow is a magnificent bird, quite as handsome as the larger raven, and suffers an injustice from its common name which is not related to any special addiction to carrion as a diet but is a corruption of its proper name, *Corvus corone*.

Phillip was a bird of great charm, and the species make better pets than the other corvids, as they are not destructive and show no interest in bright objects. The thieving habits of magpies and jackdaws are undoubtedly tiresome, lovable as the birds themselves may be.

The two young jackdaws who were his contemporaries settled down together in an outdoor aviary. They perched side by side to be hand-fed alternately ; they preened in unison, and if one had a bath the other hopped into the water as soon as he had finished.

Mimicry, vocal and physical, is strongly developed

in all birds. The desire to preen or bathe is particularly infectious, rather as the yawn of one person can set off a whole roomful of people. This can be very useful from the point of view of settling a newcomer. Actions and reactions could be followed all round the cages, aviaries and enclosures that were in sight of each other. A gull would start dipping and fluttering in an earthenware sink—then Phillip plunged into his pie-dish. A thrush began showering bath-water round its cage ; a collection of finches in an aviary awaiting release would join in—and so on throughout the community. Preening and the noon-day sleep followed the same pattern.

When the jackdaws were feeding themselves, the time came to offer them their liberty, and so I left the aviary door open one fine and sunny morning. The tamer of the two, known as Currant, hopped out and flew on to the roof and spent the day there. The other, called Chestnut after the surname of his rescuer, flew over the housetops and disappeared. When he failed to return at nightfall, I thought he had gone for good, but he was back in time for breakfast the next day, and very anxious for the aviary door to be opened—although he had been supplied with food outside. Since then, neither of the birds has taken advantage of opportunities for freedom.

I have had the same experience with small perching birds and even with sea-gulls, and it is as well to remember this before commiserating with birds in a zoo.

In the wild, birds have the satisfactions of courtship and reproduction, and many show enjoyment in the act of flying; but the other side of the coin depicts a life that is short and hard won. Food is a permanent and desperate need, and so is the maintenance of a territory in which to live and find that food. Our song birds are more often risking laryngitis in order to defend their property than voicing mere *joie de vivre*.

In even balder terms, two-thirds of the young birds hatched in one year will be dead by the following spring, and the remainder take the places of adults that have died meanwhile, thus maintaining a more or less constant population able to survive on the food supplies available in a given area.

Any poetic conceptions of life in the wild disposed of, one may consider the tame bird, cared for in a proper manner, in a somewhat different light ; but this does not mean that I have any sympathy with trappers of wild birds. It cannot be ethical to capture any kind of wild life and keep it in confinement, unless it is for the purpose of establishing a collection for scientific or educational ends.

But, once tamed and provided with the best possible conditions, most pet birds are more than content with their lot ; which is as well, for the present course of events leads one to suppose that a few generations hence many species of our wild-life will be extinct in a countryside bisected with arterial roads and drenched in insecticide sprays ; when the survivors will be able to exist only in national parks and the aviaries of zoological gardens.

CHAPTER FIVE : TO CURE SOMETIMES

OF the physician's three ancient precepts, *To cure sometimes*, *To relieve often*, *To comfort always*, the amateur bird doctor can usually hope to achieve little more than the first. Even today we know so little about what makes a bird ' tick ' that treating it as a patient must be a matter of trial and error, and the onus for weighting the scales one way or another rests in the last resort with the bird itself. If it decides to live, then it will live under the most fantastic conditions.

A classic example of this was shown by a robin that lived and bred for three seasons while carrying a sliver of wood diagonally through its body ; by some unknown mischance the point had penetrated the bird's breast and emerged from the middle of its back, having miraculously by-passed the vital organs.

The cage-bird enthusiast has problems enough when illness strikes one of his pets, but cage-birds are at least tame and accustomed to human hands. Nursing wild birds presents the additional problem of fear, which must be conquered if the patient is to be treated at all. But this is not so difficult, because of an inexplicable bond that often springs up between humans and birds ; an odd affinity that, obviously, owes nothing to any physical likeness but may be due to the avian capacity for extra-sensory perception (otherwise telepathy), which has recently been put forward as an explanation of many hitherto unexplained mysteries of bird behaviour. I believe this to be true. The amazing aerial evolutions of a flock of dunlin are more easily understood on the basis of control by a so-called mass mind.

Some people have an unconscious horror of birds that is outwardly unnoticeable, but is discernible by the hypersensitive individual bird, giving it a feeling of unease which it expresses in wildness. Other people with the best will in the world lack the imagination and experience that would give them enough confidence to handle the delicate bundles of palpitating feathers. But the average person with a gentle touch will find birds easy to manage after a little practice. Confidence inspires confidence, and slow decisive movements and a calm voice will soothe the wildest breast.

By establishing a small-scale home clinic for wild birds, one can make a very real contribution to local conservancy, and at the same time have unique opportunities for studying various species at close range. Most children are interested in a bird hospital and soon learn how to collect casualties and bring them for treatment without inflicting further damage, and this gives them a new sense of responsibility towards all animals—a lesson that is absent from the curriculum of the average school.

I have kept a record of birds treated over a period of several years, detailing the symptoms, the action taken to cure them, the diet and the final result. This list shows a steady upgrade from a miserable ten per cent to a present ratio of eighty per cent of patients completely recovered and released.

Whatever our views on birds in cages, it must be admitted that without the cage-bird keeper and the manufacturers who supply his demands, the care of wild birds in temporary captivity would be very much more difficult than it actually is. Packaged seeds, insectivorous and rearing-foods are readily obtainable nowadays, and with modern deep-freeze methods it is even possible to feed sea birds from a carton in an emergency.

Gone are the days I squeamishly remember when mashing earthworms, insects and hard-boiled egg and biscuit-meal was a daily task. Now I have a larder of packages that provide for the arrival of almost any species of bird.

Rearing baby birds is a reasonably easy business when a little skill has been acquired. Nursing accident victims is more difficult. In this case one has to deal with broken bones, the possibility of internal injuries, the effects of shock and the bird's own choice between living and dying.

I experienced an odd example of this with two sea-gulls. The first arrived with a broken wing, which after a couple of weeks was mending nicely ; then the second one arrived, outwardly undamaged but clearly very sick. I put them together in a comfortable pen, thinking that the sight of each other would be an encouragement, but I have never been so wrong. Within half a day number two was dead, reasonably enough of internal haemorrhage as autopsy showed, but soon afterwards gull number one was in a coma and died. There was no practical explanation for its death beyond some strange telepathic ' death-wish ' infection. So I learned to keep the chronically ill separate from the convalescents.

A high percentage of accidents result in broken legs and wings. Other than fracture cases, the general run of accident victims are suffering from shock and minor injuries, and they often recover with no active help on our part. What they need is safety from predators, a supply of good food and absolute quiet : in these surroundings they can, metaphorically, lick their wounds and mend themselves.

In all cases the sands of time are running out during the period from the moment disaster strikes to the arrival of the bird for treatment. The peculiar hollow structure of bird bones makes them susceptible to exposure to air in the case of serious fracture and, besides this, the effects of shock are busily at work. This time-lag has accounted for a large proportion of my twenty per cent of failures, but it is an uncontrollable feature of the work that has to be accepted.

Another question to be faced squarely is whether a case is hopeless. A too sentimental approach can result in real cruelty, and I make myself kill quite a number of maimed birds, much as I hate doing it. There are three types of casualty : the first has every prospect of complete recovery ; the second is badly injured and in obvious distress ; and the third has a good chance of recovery but will never be fit to return to the wild.

It is important to make an honest assessment as soon as a bird arrives, destroying it promptly if it falls into the second category, and choosing the common-sense and humane alternative for a bird that can only spend its future in an aviary. Some will flourish and live contentedly under these conditions, but for others such a life is out of the question. Swallows and swifts are an example : they are built for an entirely aerial existence ; indeed, swifts even sleep and mate while airborne. Keeping such birds in permanent captivity would be most unkind, and the same applies to ocean birds, like auks and petrels ; but a gull will settle down happily to a domesticated life, and so, surprisingly, will some of the waders.

The final decision must be tempered by the facilities one has for keeping a species in suitable surroundings, or the possibility of its being acceptable to a zoo with properly designed enclosures. The maxim should always be, *when in doubt, destroy.*

Various methods of destruction are recommended, but I have found that the only quick and sure means is to give the bird a sharp blow on the base of the skull, which procures an instant and painless death. Anaesthesia in any form is unsuitable for birds, as they resist it and die slowly and unpleasantly.

To return to the birds with a future, the housing

question is important. In most places passerines will form the majority of patients, and these will do well in box cages of the type used by canary and budge-rigar fanciers. Wire fronts, fitted with doors, can be bought at pet stores or corn merchants and attached to the open side of wooden packing-cases, and these will make good temporary quarters for many of the smaller species ; or one can, of course, buy these cages ready-made at a price. A useful size is about two feet long, by one foot wide, by eighteen inches high, as this will be suitable for any sick bird up to the size of a pigeon.

Many people make the mistake of giving a bird patient too much freedom, turning it loose in an attic or shed, where it will do nothing but damage itself in attempts to escape. What it needs is a shaded and restricted compartment which impresses it as a sanctuary and, strange as it may seem, a small box cage makes a frightened and bewildered bird settle down in a very short time. All-wire pet-bird cages are quite unsuitable, as they appear to be prisons from which the bird may escape if it can only batter its way through the bars.

Perches are usually arranged so that they rest on the first cross-bar of the cage front, but for the new arrival all but one should be removed, and this fixed about one inch above the floor. Food and water pots must be inside, and if the cage is fitted with outside feeders, these should be removed and the pop-holes blocked.

4

If the bird is ill enough to spend its time sitting
on the cage floor, it will appreciate a soft bed of rags
or meadow hay ; but if it is able to perch, the floor
can be littered with either sawdust or peat moss for
insectivores, and dry sand for seed-eaters. All species,
except birds of prey, need grit in order to digest their
food, and if this is not provided as a floor covering,
it should be available in a separate container.

Curiosity is strongly developed in birds, and their
investigations will soon teach them how to use glass
and plastic water founts clipped to the bars of the
cage. These are excellent appliances and can be
obtained at most pet stores. All my perching birds
have learned to use them within twenty-four hours,
and one blackbird enjoyed watching the air bubbles
rising in the tube so much that she drank enormous
amounts of water every day.

Cages for larger birds, such as a rook, should be
of the same design but of rabbit-hutch proportions.
Sea birds can rest for the first few days in a basket
or tea chest, bedded with soft hay, and then convalesce out of doors in a wire-netting run. Old,
shallow, kitchen sinks are usually to be begged, or
bought for a few shillings, from a builder's yard,
and these make good ponds for water birds.

The design and construction of aviaries depends
largely on the question of finance. It is essential to
have some kind of enclosure where the patients can
be rehabilitated before release, and provided it is
about six feet in height and allows shelter and room

for flying-exercise, the other dimensions are a matter for individual choice. In fact, I made a useful small aviary out of odd lengths of timber quartering, a few planks and five yards of half-inch wire netting, at a cost of little more than thirty shillings.

Equipped with two or three cages, an aviary and an open enclosure, the bird hospital is established, but there is still the catering department to consider. I keep two basic foods which suit all adult passerines : the first is a Dutch product called Sluisfood, and this will be eaten by most insectivores ; the second is Capern's Finch Mixture, which can be given to sparrows and buntings, as well as finches.

Some live food is necessary for insectivorous birds, and this can be provided in the form of meal-worms or 'gentles'. Meal-worms are clean and not too unpleasant to handle. They are the larvae of a beetle, *Tenebrio molitor*, which is found in flour mills, and an ounce of them, which can be bought at pet stores for about half a crown, will multiply in a cake tin to provide a constant supply. The tin should have a few air holes drilled in the lid, and then be filled with alternate layers of newspaper and broad bran, which is very slightly moistened from time to time.

Meal-worms are rather rich and indigestible and, for this reason, a ration of six a day is plenty for a thrush-sized bird, while a fledgling of the same type should not have more than one.

'Gentles' is a nice trade name for ordinary maggots. These are revolting creatures, although they are cleaned before being sold ; but birds love them and thrive on them, and they have the great advantage of softness, which makes them a suitable food for the smallest nestling.

These foods are a general stand-by. Some rarer bird visitors will thrive on the oddest diet when their natural one is impossible to obtain, and this calls for imagination and ingenuity.

Medical supplies are necessarily limited, and the medicine cupboard can only be a very modest affair, as antiseptics are not used for birds and there are few effective drugs available. However, it should be possible to obtain on veterinary prescription a small quantity of sulphanilamide powder, for use on wounds; and a seventeen-per-cent solution of sulphamezathine, which will often cure internal complaints of virus origin, as it is a specific for coccidiosis in poultry. It is given at the rate of one teaspoonful to a pint of water.

It is useful to collect a number of quill feathers dropped by species of birds of various sizes, as the stems can be cut off and split lengthwise to make very good splints for leg fractures. If a close fit is obtained, this kind of splint will be kept in position without bandaging or plaster, but it may be as well to bind it once round, top and bottom, with Scotch tape. The great advantage of this method is its lightness, which is an important aspect, particularly with small birds.

Unfortunately, wing injuries are the commonest accidents and the least likely to respond to treatment.

Dislocation, with local muscular damage, of the shoulder joint is, in my opinion, hopeless. Fractures of the upper and forearm are not promising either, but if treatment is not delayed these breaks *will* mend —with luck.

An injury that is often mistaken for a broken wing is subluxation of the carpal joint. For the sake of simplicity, one can look on this as a dislocated wrist, and it is often described as ' aeroplane wing '. The sufferer is grounded, and the wing tip, which supports the heaviest feathers, is twisted and useless. The treatment in this case is simple and effective : the flight feathers are clipped back as close as possible, without drawing blood, and the patient is kept caged until it moults through a new set of wing feathers. By this time the joint will, usually, have returned to normal, and after convalescence in an aviary the patient can be released.

Another type of casualty which appears serious, but can be cured, is the bird that has lost its tail. Many of them, particularly birds that hop rather than walk, lose all sense of balance, and fall over backwards every time they stand up. Blackbirds seem to be the most frequent victims of this accident, possibly in the course of hair-breadth escapes from cats. Again, the treatment is simple. All that is required is board and lodging for about four weeks, when nature will have supplied a new tail. It is odd that tails are replaced so promptly, while wing feathers can only be grown when a bird moults.

Wounds, with or without haemorrhage, should be bathed in cold water, and if necessary the plumage can be cut away to allow clean healing. The high metabolic rate of birds makes them less susceptible to local infection, and one application of sulphanilamide will be quite enough to clean a wound and promote healing. In fact, minor wounds are best left alone and, certainly, antiseptics should never be applied to a bird's skin.

Haemorrhage must, of course, be dealt with immediately. On one occasion I was called urgently to a neighbour's pigeon which had severed a vein in its leg. The distracted owners were bathing it in a bowl of warm water, which was rapidly filling with the bird's life-blood. I took it from them and held the leg under the cold-water tap for a few seconds, which allowed a clot to form, and the bleeding stopped. We then applied sulphanilamide powder and put the now very weak pigeon in a darkened cage. It was given milk to drink, ordinary corn, and one tablet of a proprietary brand of pigeon tonic every day for ten days, and then it was fit to return to its companions in the loft.

Long-billed birds often damage their beaks and, as a general rule, accidents of this kind are totally crippling and the sufferer should be destroyed. Only the horny tip of a bill is capable of regeneration. This is always growing to make good the wear and tear of use, and sometimes one finds rogue growth in budge-rigars and in wild soft-bills, such as starlings and blackbirds. In wild birds, the trouble usually rights itself, but the caged budgerigar needs help in the form of objects to chew—natural branches of hardwood, cuttle-bone and such.

Like the beak, claws of captive birds often grow too long, and as clipping necessitates handling and the careful avoidance of blood vessels, it is much easier to rasp the claws by glueing a strip of coarse sandpaper to the underside of one or two perches, so that a bird gives itself a manicure every time it grips the perch.

Occasionally one finds a patient with symptoms for which there is no certain diagnosis. A few years ago a number of birds were found with a leg paralysed and held at right angles to the body. I had a robin in this condition, and I gave him no treatment beyond the normal one of quiet and good food. He gradually recovered and spent his convalescence in a spare room, where he perched or squatted on a radiator, glorying in the heat and possibly gaining some therapeutic effect from it.

A vitamin deficiency affects young waterfowl with leg paralysis, and this will respond to doses of cod-liver oil and vitamin B complex, which can be supplied in the form of yeast extract. I have known a young heron to suffer in this way, as well as ducklings and cygnets, and these birds are often destroyed in the mistaken belief that they are beyond aid.

This chapter of accidents must end with the saddest casualty of all : the victim of scientific farming and horticulture.   These poisoned birds are generally in the throes of convulsions when they are found, and there is only one thing to do—kill them instantly.

A correspondent in the United States tells me that yeast extract will sometimes save a bird that has taken a mild dose of insecticide, but so far all my cases have been severe and hopeless.

Few species are safe from these poisons.   Finches pick it up from dressed seeds at sowing-time ; so do mice and voles, which are then eaten by birds of prey ;   while insectivorous birds are certain victims in areas sprayed with DDT or other toxic chemicals. Besides birds, other creatures like hedgehogs, shrews, snakes and lizards, and even foxes, badgers and stoats and weasels are potential victims.

As an example, an earthworm which has eaten material containing DDT will accumulate the poison, and when it in turn is eaten by a thrush, the bird will again accumulate this dose and add to it as other polluted insects are digested.   This collected poison gradually invades its whole body until the brain cells are reached.   Then death mercifully follows locomotor paralysis and convulsions.

CHAPTER SIX : FIRE AND WATER

I KNEW nothing about the fire until a group of small boys arrived at the door, holding a cardboard shoe-box containing five fledgling meadow pipits. They had taken the birds from a smouldering branch, left by the fire as it was drawn towards the centre of the conflagration. The month was June and we had been without rain for weeks : an ideal time to clear from a piece of scrub-land the few rabbits that had managed to survive myxomatosis.

In the evening I carried the box of little birds back to the scene of the fire, which had burnt out to leave an area of blackened and still smoking desolation. I set the box down near a tussock of grass, walked away for about fifty yards, and then waited. Realising that they were alone, the young pipits began to call, and after a while they were answered from a distance. Then a pair of adult birds landed in a nearby hedge, their thin voices calling urgently, ' *tseep tissip* '. At this the fledglings left the box and made for the shelter of a blackthorn where the parent birds were perched. A tremendous reunion ensued and I left them to it.

The next day I walked over the burnt, now cool, ground. Nothing remained but blackened stumps of furze bushes and red patches where the earth had

baked into brick dust. Near several of the charred
stumps white skeletons crouched, falling to powder
at the touch of a finger ; but of the larks, the warblers
and all but seven of the pipits, which had been nesting there, there was no sign ; their bones were too
small and brittle to leave a memorial as the rabbits
had done.

The wholesale destruction of furze, thorn and
brambles had brought to light a deep pond, the
size of an average swimming-pool, which had lain
forgotten in their midst. Like its surroundings, the
pond was barren all through that summer, but on
a wild February day next year I was attracted
towards it by an odd sound, half-way between a
quack and a whistle, which was like the voice of
a wigeon and yet not quite the same. The sound
was the croaking of toads.

I stood at the water's edge and looked at the toads,
and about two hundred golden eyes returned my stare
from under the water. They had a mad, dedicated
look ; each toad sitting on the mud a few inches below
the surface of the pond, waiting and watching, all
facing shorewards ; all croaking intermittently.

They were waiting for the females of the party to
arrive. A number of male toads always get to the
breeding-pond first ; the females travel from their
hibernation quarters at a more leisurely pace, largely
independent but sometimes meeting—and then carrying on their backs—a late male who has joined the
overland trek. A thousand or more of these strange

creatures may crawl for anything up to two miles in order to reach a certain pond, even by-passing other stretches of water which appear quite as suitable breeding-grounds. It is thought that they always return to their place of birth, and some naturalists are experimenting with metal-alloy tags which will show the extent of these annual migratory movements.

As this toad pond lay near a walk I took every day while exercising my dogs, I watched the course of events, at first with mild interest and then with fascinated horror, because the placid pool was soon the scene of appalling carnage.

The first dozen or so female toads to reach the water were instantly seized by all the waiting males, so that some disappeared in the midst of a mass of struggling bodies and sank in deep water, where all of them drowned. Others with only three or four suitors to support made desperate attempts to swim to the surface with their loads, taking gulps of air before sinking exhausted for the last time. Soon the pond was like some weird submarine battlefield, the bottom littered with ghostly white bodies, which shimmered as refracted light penetrated the water to outline them against the black mud.

Only the late arrivals were able to lay their eggs, tangling the gelatinous strings of spawn among the water-weeds, and then departing as quickly as they had come ; leaving me somewhat disillusioned with a *Wind in the Willows* view of the private life of a toad.

That year the winter weather carried on into early

spring, and the coast was swept by gales and high seas. This brought a number of casualties, the most serious of which was a black-headed gull. In normal circumstances I would have destroyed the bird, as it had been thrown against overhead wires by the wind, and this had fractured the ulna and dislocated the ' wrist ' of one wing, and dislocated a leg on the same side. Against my judgement, I decided to try and mend what appeared to be a hopeless case, because its rescuers had driven nearly twenty miles through the dark countryside in order to bring it to me.

The first job was to clip away all the feathers on the damaged wing, carefully judging where it was safe to cut across the larger quills without severing the blood vessels. This done, a wooden splint padded with cotton-wool was laid along the underside of the fractured upper arm, and bound in place with adhesive tape. The leg was then set in a similar splint, as I had no quill splints of a suitable size ; and that was all I could do.

The gull was kept quiet for the first few days, and then allowed out in a garden pen. She settled down remarkably well, and I was able to remove the leg splints in a week, and in four weeks the fractured wing bone had set, too. The aeroplane-wing symptoms remained, but I had to hope for the best over this.

In fact, a complete cure took eight months, but when she did go she flew away across the bay without a backward glance. An adult herring gull, which had shared her pen from the day in August when it was brought in smothered in fuel oil, only stayed for twelve weeks, but returned frequently until a cold and foodless reception drove it back to a proper way of life.

That same stormy spring brought two rarities, and I found them both on the same day. The first was a little auk, which had struggled out of the sea to die among the tide-wrack ; it was still warm when I picked it up, but utterly dead. Some few drops of oil were spattered across its breast, but otherwise it appeared unharmed. Evidently a mere teaspoonful of fuel oil is enough to make these small birds prey to the elements.

Although I knew that little auks were tiny, I was surprised at the size of this one as it lay in the palm of my hand ; a razorbill in miniature, with a stubby beak rather like that of a bullfinch. It was sad to think that this bird had braved a journey from the Arctic to be wrecked on the comparatively mild shores of north Devon.

In a field near the toad pond I met the second of the day's casualties, and it was an odd meeting. I saw this little grey bird running towards me when it was still some distance away, and told the dogs to lie down and wait. The bird came on, and when it was at my feet I stooped and picked it up, holding it in cupped hands. It made no attempt to escape, and I was able to carry it home without any trouble.

The bird was a grey phalarope and another traveller, this time *en route* for the polar basin from its winter quarters in the south Atlantic, where it lives at sea in the region of the equator. This is an almost entirely pelagic species, which seldom comes ashore except to breed in the tundras of the Arctic.

The behaviour of this individual told me that it was in a desperate condition. Once, when I was a child, I had seen a grey squirrel behave in the same way, and still remember the wonder and the tragedy of this episode. I was wandering through a wood near my home when the squirrel came scampering through some undergrowth and allowed itself to be picked up. It was quite without fear, sitting on my shoulders and climbing over my coat as I hurried back to show the family this new and charming pet. It was just as tame in the house, exploring the sitting-room and then coming back to curl up on my knee. I was a little concerned because it showed no interest in food, but I put this down to the excitement of its new surroundings ; certainly it never dawned on me that this wild squirrel was behaving in a very curious and ominous manner, and this made the shock of finding it stone-cold and quite dead the next morning all the more terrible. Whoever had shot the animal had been almost out of range, but one or two pellets had perforated its stomach, and these had been enough to bring about a slow, but apparently painless, death. Whether animals and birds sensing impending death seek comfort from a larger creature, as a kind of wishful return to the nest and its security, is a question one cannot answer.

The phalarope followed the same pattern. It settled quite happily in a large shallow box littered with earth, drank from a glass dish of water, and toyed rather aimlessly with one or two small earth-worms. I thought it would probably eat if it was left alone, and hoped that there was a chance for its recovery, as it was uninjured and only suffering from exhaustion and lack of food. But the next morning it was dead.

I saw grey phalaropes now and again afterwards. They paused in the bay to feed while on passage to and from the north, and when the tide was high and the water calm they would come inshore to within a yard of the sea's edge : swimming buoyantly and giving characteristic spins at intervals to churn up the sandy bottom and, with it, the lurking shrimps and other small marine life. In appearance they are very like many of the commoner little waders which run about the shore and mud-flats, probing, chirruping and flying in formation, wheeling across the water as if controlled by a single thought ; but whereas the phalarope is an expert swimmer, these waders will drown out of their depth.

Another difference which sets it apart is the domestic life of a grey phalarope. The male is the drab one of the pair, while his mate adorns herself in gay breeding-plumage ; and she remains a gadabout, leaving the care of the eggs and chicks entirely to her truly henpecked spouse.

Waders, with a chance of recovery from some

accident, do remarkably well in captivity, as they are intelligent and become tame very easily. But they do present problems for the inexperienced. My first bird of this type was a snipe suffering from a broken wing, which I splinted with some difficulty, as holding an energetic snipe is rather like trying to compress a steel spring.

But I succeeded in the end, and put the bird in a large box cage littered with earth, grass clippings and moss. The length of its bill demanded deep food and water bowls, and these were made of glass, as I find that birds are more likely to take food which is clearly visible. The food bowl was filled with earth and water to the consistency of thick cream, to which was added a writhing bunch of earthworms. The snipe understood this mode of feeding at once, and probed the mud eagerly until its sensitive bill tip found a worm, which was then sucked up like liquid being drawn into a hypodermic syringe. The bird ate its fill and seemed completely at home in these strange conditions, thriving as the days passed and, clearly, with every prospect of a full recovery.

But I had not taken into account the capacity for jumping of these long-legged birds. If one watches a disturbed snipe take off from a bog, it appears to rocket into the air as if from a catapult ; and, in a sense, this is what really happens, because its legs propel it off the ground rather as the spring of a clay-pigeon trap. It is, in fact, well airborne before the wings begin to flap.

As my bird became stronger, it decided to try to fly, and, taking off in the usual manner, broke its neck when the wooden roof of the cage intervened. I should have imagined that this might happen, and blamed myself for it ; but these lessons in the care of animals are all too often learned the hard way, and it did serve as a guide to the correct treatment of my next patient.

Not so long ago that extraordinary bird, the ruff, bred regularly in Britain, but nowadays it is only a visitor and extinct as a breeding species. Why this should be so is not clear, as it has not suffered from the mechanisation of agriculture which is wiping out our indigenous corncrakes and quail. But, whatever the reason, the sight of a ruff in the west country is very unusual indeed.

It was, therefore, some days after its arrival before I reached the inescapable conclusion that I was housing a ruff in my aviary. One is inclined to fall over backwards disproving the rarity of a bird, even when the recognition signs are obvious !

The bird arrived, as so many other patients have done, in the hands of a boy. He and a friend had seen it running about on a marsh some two miles away, and after catching it had walked back with the frenzied bird enclosed in a cap. They thought it was a snipe and I, at first sight, took it for a young greenshank.

This was another case in which I had to equate the bird's prospects with the amount of trouble its rescuers had taken. I have often had to kill birds which have been brought in by children, carefully explaining where humanity ends and sentimental cruelty begins ; but whenever possible their protégés are treated, if there is the remotest chance for them.

These boys expected me to do something for this unknown wader and I had to decide on a drastic measure. The left wing was smashed in two places, and only attached to the body by ligaments and some muscle, and so the only course was amputation. While one boy held the bird and the other held its wing tip, I steeled myself and, after tying a ligature of clean string next to the shoulder, cut off the wing with one snip of sharp scissors. The boy who now had the amputated wing in his hand turned a slightly green face towards me and asked what he should do with it. I said briskly that it could be left on the floor for the moment, and we must now settle the bird in an aviary and feed it.

The three of us trooped out into the garden, one still carrying the bird, which was the only member of the party that appeared quite unaffected by the operation. While I filled a glass photographic developing-dish with water to make a pond for it, the boys dug up some small earthworms, which we added to the water. To their delight the bird began feeding at once, and we left it alone to eat and recover from its ordeal.

I was very doubtful about its prospects, but hoped for the best. Each morning I went out expecting to find a corpse in the aviary, and every time the little wader looked stronger and was tamer. Within three days it would eat out of a dish held in my hand, and take meal-worms from my fingers.

The wing stump had not bled at all and the ligature was still in place, and I decided to leave it until it dropped off as the skin shrivelled and healed, because the less handling the bird had to put up with the better.

Most waders naturally eat a variety of foods, and I wanted this one to learn that other things besides live food were edible, even if they looked odd at first sight. I made up a mixture of a brand of tinned cat food (containing pressure-cooked fish and bones, and boiled barley), with Sluisfood and meal-worms, and offered this in a flat glass dish. The wriggling meal-worms were taken first, and in picking them up, the bird tasted the other food and ate it with evident relish. Later, when I knew that it was a ruff, I added a spoonful of finch-mixture seeds to its diet.

I spent hours with a pile of reference books, permutating the colour of its plumage, its size and shape, the length of bill and legs and their colour ; finding that a sandpiper was just that much different, so was a knot and a dunlin ; while a greenshank was bigger and had a slightly up-tilted bill. There was no doubt that I had a ruff, or more likely the female of the species, a reeve. To make its identity absolutely certain, the bird began to answer a jackdaw in a neighbouring aviary, calling with a rather harsh note, ' *too-whit* '.

In the moment of decision when the bird arrived, I had thought that it could find a home, if it recovered, in the wader enclosures of one of our larger zoos ; but as time went on I found that it was quite content with the accommodation I had to offer, and so I planned to keep it and, in the course of time, try to borrow a mate from a zoo.

The home life of a ruff is not very respectable ; in fact, they are entirely promiscuous and the male never sets eyes on his offspring. In the breeding-season the ruffs gather at a communal courting-ground, which is known as a ' lek ' ; and here they cavort, engage in mock battles, and display their brightly coloured neck ruffs and ear tufts. Passing reeves are attracted to this hubbub, and after watching for a while from the ring-side, accept the advances of the most importunate ruff, and then retire from the scene to nest, incubate the eggs and rear the family, in solitude.

A quite unrelated bird, the black grouse, behaves in an identical manner, and it seems strange that such a mode of courtship should evolve in two species which have entirely different habitats : one a marsh-land bird and the other a resident of old forests and the moors.

Game birds, waterfowl and waders all have the same type of chick ; it is clothed in thick down, and able to run about and pick up its own food within an hour or so of hatching from the egg.

These independent, or nidifugous, chicks are easier to rear in many ways, but on the other hand their very mobility can be a hazard. They can lose contact with the family if they wander too far, and are then certain prey for hawks and other predators, as they have no instinctive response to the shadow of wings overhead, and will only ' freeze ' at a warning-call from one of their own kind.

The parent bird must, therefore, be forever on guard to give warning of approaching danger, and some carry this to such an extreme that they defeat their own ends. An oyster-catcher has often shown me exactly where its young were hiding ; and so have a pair of ringed plovers, whose eggs were completely camouflaged on a pebble beach and would have been passed unnoticed, but for their anxiety calls and attempts to lead me away from a certain spot.

Several waders perform the broken-wing ruse. I have seen this many times, and been fascinated by an acting capacity which reproduces exactly the behaviour of a truly maimed bird.

Although I lived by an estuary which was haunted by an enormous variety of waders, very few were brought to me as casualties ; probably because their structure is so delicate that an accident is likely to kill them outright. One of the few was a curlew chick, and it was so enchanting that it might have stepped from the pages of a child's picture-book.

It had been found standing on the grass verge of a busy road, apparently dazed by a glancing blow from a car, or perhaps thrown into the hedge by the slip-stream of passing traffic. By the time it arrived with me it was recovering, and I could find no sign of injury. The obvious course was to get it back to a family group of its own kind as quickly as possible, and so I packed it into a cat-basket and drove up the hill behind the village to a sheep pasture, where I knew curlews were breeding.

I planned to loose the chick through a gate into a big field where it could join the other birds without my presence becoming known ; and I brought a camera and binoculars with me so that the scene could be watched and photographed. I badly wanted a record of a creature so clearly photogenic.

As I opened the lid of the basket the chick remained quite still, looking up at me with enormous liquid eyes. As chicks go, it was large, but covered in typical downy fluff ; sandy coloured, blotched and streaked with dark brown. The legs were awkwardly long, like a foal's, but the bill did not appear to be either as long or as down-curved as that of an adult bird.

With the camera set and everything prepared, I put the chick down in the gateway and stood back to get some pictures, but I had reckoned without the little bird's reaction to a view of freedom. It went off up the field with the loping strides of an ostrich, cheeping as it went, until near the headland it got an answering call and flurried back to a family life once more.

My feeling of relief was stronger than one of regret

for a missed photograph. From my point of view, the nidifugous chick has this tremendous advantage in that it is possible to farm it out on any family of its own species. The parents do not distinguish one chick from another ; I have so often seen domestic hens interchange their broods, and had one old hen who always collected everyone else's chickens, trying to spread herself into a canopy that would cover about thirty burrowing, chirping bundles of fluff, while the other mothers had to content themselves with one or two offspring that had remained faithful.

CHAPTER SEVEN : YOUNG VISITORS

WHILE treating accident victims is very much more difficult, the nursery department is perhaps the most fascinating and rewarding side of wild-bird care. Young birds are easily tamed, and soon learn to accept a human being as a large and ungainly parent, perching on a forefinger and looking up to meet the eyes of this enormous creature, who provides odd but tasty food and tries to chirrup with such discordant results.

An immediate meal of suitable food is the first consideration for a newly arrived patient, as every one, whether it is a fledgling or an injured adult, will be suffering from starvation more than anything else.

Baby birds carry a distinctive mark until they are old enough to fend for themselves : the gaping capacity of the bill is enlarged at each side by fleshy lips, often yellow in colour, so that the parent can thrust food down the gullet. As the baby grows the lips gradually shrivel until they finally disappear altogether and the bird can be termed a young adult. This insignia of babyhood is a most valuable guide for the hand-rearer, who can see at a glance what stage the youngster has reached and when it should be taught to feed itself.

Given a chance, young birds will go on begging

for food for long after they are quite capable of picking it out of a dish for themselves ; and then, in the same manner as parent birds, one must harden the heart and begin to ignore its protests, while leaving a dish of food within reach. Hunger will do the rest.

The genuinely helpless baby needs a lot of care and frequent feeds. The frequency is at first sight appalling, but three meals during each hour of daylight are only needed in the initial stages, and at this time, watching the rate of growth and feathering is so interesting that the work involved seems very worth while.

Nestlings, who need warmth as well as food, are fortunately rare customers, because if their parents are killed or desert the nest for any reason, the babies die almost at once of cold and hunger.

Once, some children brought me a naked nestling, which had hatched somewhat precipitously when its egg had fallen from a tree on to the road beneath. This can happen when a clumsy parent leaves the nest, but the chick rarely survives the fall.

This one was full of life, but so immature that it was impossible to identify it with certainty. It was grotesque in appearance, like all helpless chicks : enormous eyes visible under the blinding but semi-transparent lids and surrounding skin ; a long stringy neck, and a bulbous body from which the legs and wings projected like match-sticks stuck in a potato. The transparency of its skin showed the inner working of its body with extraordinary clarity, and it was possible to follow its digestive processes from, so to speak, end to end.

A particularly interesting aspect of this bird was the 'egg-tooth' attached to the upper mandible of its bill. This shows another example of the relationship between birds and reptiles. All bird embryos and the young of egg-laying snakes and lizards are equipped with an egg-tooth ; in Britain these reptiles are represented by the grass snake and sand lizard (our other snakes and lizards give birth to live young). This calcic eruption is not a true tooth, but is provided as a means of breaking the egg-shell so that the young can emerge, and within a few days of hatching it disappears.

I failed to keep this nestling alive for more than five days, but succeeded with another that was only a little older, because I then had the advantage of knowing its species and was able to feed it correctly.

It was a house-sparrow—naked, cold and scarcely breathing—which had been brought in a cardboard box from a neighbouring town. At first sight it was not promising, but I thought that if it could be warmed there might be a chance ; and so I spent the next hour one-handed, holding the clammy little bird in the other and eating my lunch with a fork. Gradually I became less aware of its coldness and then, suddenly, it gave a convulsive wriggle and chirped.

I opened my palm and offered a morsel of scrambled egg. The nestling gaped hungrily, waving its ugly blind head, which seemed to be attached to its body by a neck made of string and cellophane, and as the food was swallowed one could see it descending into the crop like a lift going down to the ground floor.

The crop began to bulge alarmingly with its yellow contents and I decided that it was time to stop ; and, bedding the horrid scrap of pulsating life that hoped to be a sparrow in a handkerchief-lined box, I put it to keep warm in the linen-cupboard.

Next day one bleary eye had opened and the nestling was feeding regularly ; the sight of my hand initiated an instant response, and he soon knew the sound of my voice, too ; so that if I talked to the family in his hearing I would be interrupted by angry cheeping from the depths of the cupboard.

Such a character needed a name and he was called Frankenstein, but, in time, this was shortened to Frankie as his appearance began to improve. First he grew some wing feathers, then a little down appeared on the shoulders and the top of his head, and then a few quills sprouted to represent a tail ; and soon he stopped looking like a miniature ptero-dactyl and was able to scramble about his hand-kerchief nest and even climb on to my open hand.

In this case imprinting was inevitable and the focus of his affection was, and still is, my hand ; in which, so to speak, he had been reborn. He liked it to be held loosely clenched so that he could burrow about inside, poking his head out between my fingers and then darting in again, and finally settling down for a snooze. At this age he was little more than an inch and a half in length, and it seemed incredible that anything so minute could have such a personality.

As he became more active I allowed him more freedom, when I had time. He loved to run about the lawn, catching insects among the grass stems, but always with an eye on my hand, which had to be laid on the ground, palm up, so that he could take refuge in it if another bird came in sight. If I crawled across the lawn, trailing a hand and calling his name, Frankie followed, chirping frantically until he caught up with me.

After about three weeks he was gradually weaned from the warmth of his airing-cupboard retreat, and learned to sleep on a perch in a box cage. At the same time he began to feed himself from a dish of brown bread and milk, but still liked to beg for special titbits. Brown bread, made crumbly moist with milk, was his staple diet, and to this was added a little cooked egg, and the interior of one meal-worm a day.

The skin of meal-worms is rather tough and likely to be too indigestible for young birds of the smaller species ; and so I cut off the head of the larva to kill it, and then squeeze out the white inside, which is sickeningly like toothpaste but caviare for a bird.

All the young of seed-eating birds are fed on insects and other soft foods for the first weeks of their lives, and the bill is not hard enough to crack seeds until they are about three months old, when the yellow lips of baby-hood have disappeared. Frankie made several attempts before he was able to husk his first seed, but once this was achieved he preferred finch mixture to childish milk sop, and was almost grown-up.

The intelligence of sparrows is widely recognised, but just how much they are able to learn is, I think, still underrated. Before he was fully fledged Frankie had learned to pull a toy truck up an incline by haul-ing on a piece of string, thus obtaining a prize of bread ; and he knew the meal-worm tin by sight and began to chirrup and flutter his wings if I came into the room carrying it.

Owing to his unnatural start in life, Frankie would not have survived if he had been released to fend for himself, and so he has remained a family pet.

Other sparrows have come and gone, arriving as lost fledglings, and after a short stay, ending with an educational spell in an aviary, joining their raucous kind in freedom. Some were especially endearing : there was Vermintrude, who still lives in a friend's garden, recognisable by a yellow celluloid ring attached to her leg ; and Urchin, who slept indoors at night for several weeks after his release, and two years later was still popping in at the kitchen window to filch food for his own young.

I have put celluloid rings on most of my birds before their release, because this is the only way of proving whether or not hand-reared birds can survive without proper parental education. Results have shown that they can and do, but unfortunately, in common with an enormous number of their truly wild brethren, a proportion fall victims to prowling cats.

If one is interested in the personality of birds, it is inevitable that the most intelligent will prove the most attractive, and it is a sad fact that almost all the birds possessing a sense of curiosity and an aptitude for solving puzzles, which can only be explained in terms of intelligence, are at odds with the economics of the human race and, in consequence, classed as vermin. Sparrows are one example ; crows another ; and the wood-pigeon is now, justifiably, labelled Farm Enemy Number One.

I have always liked pigeons and doves, which are one family, *Columbidae*, divided by the comparative length of their tails—the dove generally has a long tail graduated towards the tip, whereas a pigeon's tail is shorter and level.

There are four species commonly found in Britain : the stock dove, which is very like a wood-pigeon but lacks the familiar white markings ; the rock dove, distinguished as the ancestor of most varieties of domestic pigeons ; the delinquent wood-pigeon itself, otherwise called the ring dove ; and the turtle dove, whose sleepy voice is heard locally where there are woods and orchards. A new arrival from the Continent, which is steadily increasing in a few parts of the country, is the collared turtle dove.

Our village appears to lie across the homeward route of a great many racing-pigeons, because every

year a number of them make a landfall in the neigh-
bourhood, too exhausted to fly on ; and so when I
was asked to come and see an injured pigeon, I took
it for granted that the patient would be a homer.
The bird was in a wire-netting-covered apple box
and, when I looked inside, there was a miserable
object, a wood-pigeon squab with a large wound
extending across its breast and under one wing. It
stared up at me in piteous fright and there was no
question about what I must do.

When we got home I examined the pathetic little
bird more closely. The wound was a tear, probably
made by the claws of a cat, and it had been smeared
with Stockholm tar by the rescuer (who kept poultry
and used the tar as a dressing for hens suffering from
the cannibalistic attentions of their fellows) ; this
seemed to me to be rather drastic treatment for a
nestling pigeon, and so I removed as much as possible
with daubs of butter. Whether an ointment made
from butter and Stockholm tar promotes healing, or
the bird's own metabolism went to work in spite
of it, the result was that, once it was able to feed
and rest quietly without fear, it began to mend
rapidly.

Food was the real problem. Parent pigeons feed
their young on a gruel-like liquid known as ' milk ',
which is produced by glandular secretions in the crop.
The squab has a gristle-soft bill which it thrusts into
the gaping throat of the parent, who pumps the
' milk ' up to it by muscular contractions of the neck,

allowing the young bird to drink its fill. As the baby grows, its diet gradually alters, so that it gets a mixture of ' milk ' and part-digested vegetable matter and grains, and then the secretions cease and it learns to eat adult food.

Reproducing this kind of diet and mode of feeding is difficult, to say the least of it, and particularly in the case of a bird that is frightened out of its wits by human beings. I spent a patient but hopeless half-hour trying to reassure the squab and persuade it to take food from my fingers ; and then remembered a childhood ability to make a noise in my throat which sounded like a cross between a gargle and a purr, and which I had thought resembled the cooing of doves. I must have been right, because the squab's response was instantaneous : it stood up and peered into my face, squeaking like an excited mouse, its wings quivering.

It was difficult to distract it from my face, where the coos came from, and draw its attention to my hand, which I held loosely clenched, leaving a circular hole between the thumb and forefinger ; but in the end, it began to burrow its head into my hand and to suck down the gruel I was holding. This was a mixture of an egg and biscuit-meal food intended for rearing canaries, stirred into enough cow's milk to make a kind of railway-hotel porridge.

Evidently young pigeons pay no regard to the appearance of their parents and rely entirely on vocal contact, because once I made a suitable noise I

Gilly

' Teasing was his special line '

' He began to show symptoms
of sunning display '

' All the crow tribe react to the
sun '

' Gentleness and patience will soon tame a razorbill '

'A hawk of these dimensions might have been awe-inspiring'

' The wood pigeon is
a timid and gentle
creature '

' I stood the cage by
the open window and
allowed them out '

'Gloria comes in search of me'—now look over the page
for Gloria grown up

The Author at home

became a parent pigeon and the squab was completely tame.

After the first few feeds from my hand, always accompanied by encouraging coos and responsive shrill squeaks, the bird learned to drink from a plastic egg-cup, which made the proceedings less messy; and from then on all was plain sailing, the injury healing, plumage growing and the whole bird changing from a rag-bag object into a beautiful pigeon.

If one is not blinded to its appearance by the damage it does to crops, it is clear that the wood-pigeon is one of the handsomest species on the British list. The young bird is an almost uniform pale grey in colour, even having grey legs and eyes; but, as it matures, the legs become red, a gloss of iridescent purple and emerald green pervades the feathers of its throat and breast, and the characteristic ring of white appears on the neck.

In character, the wood-pigeon is a timid and gentle creature, and if it is tamed makes a charming pet. Mine now shares a large aviary with the ruff and a number of finches, and is always gentle with any small bird, however cheeky it may be; but I am still hailed as a pigeon, the other member of a two-bird flock, and have to put up with having my hair combed and my nose pulled, and then must play my part in the business of billing and cooing by scratching the nape of its neck.

These two examples, a house-sparrow and a pigeon,

serve to illustrate the enormous variation in methods of feeding young birds employed by the parents of different families, and so it is as well to check with a text-book before embarking on trying to hand-rear an unfamiliar baby bird.

I had been trying in vain to persuade a young grey wagtail to take food, before I thought of offering a live fly buzzing in a pair of forceps. This was taken at once, and after that the little bird took Sluisfood from my fingers as a matter of course, because once the initial feed has been accepted, tameness follows automatically ; food offering and parenthood are synonymous to the avian mind.

This wagtail was a delightful creature. Its cage stood in the front porch, which is like a small conservatory, to keep it safe from the unwelcome curiosity of Orry ; and, when it had learned to feed from my hand, all human beings were looked on as friends and potential sources of food. It would beg from anyone, dancing on its perch and chirruping loudly while whoever it was searched the window-panes for a fly. This was a very popular sport with children, who found Willie irresistible.

When the time came for the bird to learn to feed itself, I provided a shallow glass dish of water and floated some swatted house-flies on the surface, and these were taken without hesitation ; but he took much longer in learning to eat from a food dish, and this shows again how important it is to imagine a form of management that will appeal to a bird's instinctive reactions, however remote from reality it may be.

I used this experience with an adult pied wagtail later on, and found that it responded just as promptly to the glass dish and the floating insects ; becoming tame remarkably quickly.

Sadly, Willie came to grief. His cage included a nest-box, which was attached outside and entered by a hole in line with one of the top perches, and he spent a lot of time popping in and out of the moss-lined nest, sleeping in it at night. One morning he was not chirping as usual, and on opening the lid of the nest-box I found him dead inside, with a broken neck.

The villain of the piece was a field-mouse, which had somehow found its way in at the front door and into Willie's nest : an intrusion that frightened the little bird and made it fly up to crash against the wooden lid in the dark. This was one of those unexpected tragedies which it is impossible to guard against.

If one keeps birds, mice are a constant problem, because they are attracted equally by seed and insecti-vorous foods. The fact that I like mice adds to my difficulties.

Conditioned at an early age by Beatrix Potter and Walt Disney, pink-sugar mice in the Christmas stock-ing and live white mice distractedly crawling about my vest—it is difficult to leave behind these impres-sionable years, to leap on a chair, yell for the cat, and set toasted-cheese-baited traps with demoniacal cunning, carrying the result away on a shovel.

At a more sophisticated age, immediately following the white-mouse era, I kept African gerbille rats (since glorified as the symbol of the Eighth Army), and one in particular, called Reggie, slept on my bed. The gerbilles flourished and multiplied until some unknown disease swept through them like wildfire, leaving a sickly Reggie as the sole survivor.

He lived for a week and then succumbed under my pillow, so that I woke to find a sad little corpse, and joined the family at breakfast red-eyed and incoherent. When the awful truth was finally understood, a visiting uncle, home on leave from the East, sprang from his chair bellowing, ' Great heavens, the filthy brute probably had bubonic plague ! '

And there my close association with rodents ended, until a few years ago when, for reasons I need not elaborate, I found myself in charge of a pair of tame mice. One was albino and the other fawn with a white tip to his tail.

In something like three months these two produced twenty-six children and things became desperate. I decided to transport the entire family to a sunny bank on some scrub-land a couple of miles away up the estuary ; but while I was collecting them all into a box, Father (the fawn one with a white tip to his tail and, by now, a chip out of one ear) escaped irrevocably into the wood-shed, and so only twenty-seven mice were taken to their new quarters ; where several months later busy white, black-and-white and fawn individuals could be seen scuttling in and out of a labyrinth of holes and runways.

A few days after the general release, my beagle came out of the wood-shed carrying a limp body, rather damp but still recognisably fawn and with a chipped ear and a white-tipped tail. That should have been the end of the dynasty, but after a while it became all too apparent that Father had spent some crowded last hours with the field-mice who used the shed as a winter retreat.

The first visible result was a pair of black mice with white spots in the middle of their foreheads ; the next were chocolate with white spots ; and then, with Mendel cast to the four winds, we ran the gamut of possible colours, culminating in a generation that was of the palest dove-grey. Only albinism was kept in abeyance.

By now, we are accustomed to having exotic-coloured mice about the place, and almost point with astonishment at any poor throw-back in drab brown ; but their charm began to wain when the lure of bird foods drew them towards the house.

When I am forced to it, I can set a trap and catch a house-mouse, and have watched with interest while Piper stalked one ; but it takes a steel heart indeed to butcher a glossy black or dove-grey mouse who sits on the draining-board washing his whiskers while you wash the dishes. The most drama-filled moment of the new mouse era was when I stopped, a split second before decanting a saucepanful of boiling water into the sink and over a black mouse very obviously *enceinte*, and near her time at that.

Over and above any liking for mice, the law of the jungle does not permit one to attack a female in this delicate condition, and so I arranged a dish-cloth as a sort of ladder out of the sink and left her to it for the night. Next morning when I came to retrieve the cloth it felt warm and abnormally heavy, and further investigation revealed a cross-faced mother and a cosy family of naked pink babies within its folds.

The dish-cloth had to be written off anyway, and so I gathered up the family, cloth and all, and put them in a box in the wood-shed, where they probably flourish today.

The untimely death of the young wagtail had long since shown that mice and small birds do not mix, and so the few mice that remained indoors were trapped ; their corpses making tasty dishes for the pet crows.

It is reasonable to expect a large measure of intelligence in birds like crows, or even in smaller species such as sparrows, but to find that a fledgling house martin could learn and respond quickly was a surprise. This little bird arrived, as usual, in a cardboard box ; its rescuer had found it lying on the garden path below a nest high in the eaves of a three-story house, and, without a fire-brigade, it would have been impossible to return the fledgling to its family.

I suspected an infestation of mite to be the cause of its leaving the nest. This often happens, particularly if the parents have found the previous year's nest intact and used it again, after carrying out minor repairs and additions, and so it is a kindness to knock down all the nests within reach once the birds have left in the late autumn.

The little martin seemed unharmed by his fall, and soon settled in a bundle of dry grass, which had been dusted with pyrethrum powder to eradicate any parasites in the bird's plumage. I tried the fly-in-forceps technique in my first attempt at feeding it, and this worked perfectly, but I wondered if a diet of house-flies would prove enough. Fortunately it did, as I could not catch midges and mosquitoes in sufficient quantity.

For the next week I seemed to spend most of my time, swat in hand, searching the walls and windows for elusive flies, for the eagerly gaping bird would eat six at a meal and ask for more. It became completely tame and liked to perch on the bookshelf at the back of my desk, unmoved by the clatter of the typewriter ; or use my finger as a launching-pad from which to take short flights.

At the end of a week I judged that it was fit enough to go free, and took it back to the path below its nest. Above us a flock of martins wheeled in the air, hunting for insects and then dropping down to visit one of the battery of mud nests attached to the wall under the eaves. I watched for a suitable moment and then held the young bird high above my head in an open hand. It hesitated for a moment before taking wing, fluttering in a halting moth-like manner which worried me, but then it heard the other martins' shrill cries in the sky and saw them swooping over the housetops, and realised the power of its own wings.

Perhaps a thermal air current helped its first soaring flight, which swept it upwards to join the throng of its kind, turning the bird that had been earth-bound in my hand a moment before into a black speck, hard to see against the clouds.

I stayed to watch for a while, and when a party of foragers returned to the eaves one flew low as if inclined to make a landing on me, but the shrill voices above called and it turned away towards them again. I was glad, and only wished the bird well on its journey thousands of miles southwards to a landfall in Africa.

These journeys are one of the greatest marvels of nature, and yet they happen so regularly, as the martins, the swallows and the swifts come and go, like the cuckoo, serving to mark the beginning and end of our seasons, that they tend to be taken for granted. But in the last few decades a number of scientists have concentrated on the mysteries of migration, and in recent years a great deal of the almost incredible truth about it has become known.

It is hard to believe that the chick of the smallest migratory bird comes out of its egg fully equipped with a knowledge of the constellations, and the ability to observe the position of the sun in relation to the time of day and to compute this with the remembered position at the same hour on its home ground.

This, in fact, means that a bird like a house-martin, five inches in length and weighing less than an ounce, must have an internal clock mechanism, a compass and a built-in sextant.

Ringing-schemes are operated in several countries to provide information on the migratory travels of birds, and have shown remarkable results. An Arctic tern ringed in Denmark was picked up in the Antarctic, 11,000 miles away ; a Manx shearwater travelled 5,000 miles in one month ; while a swift covered 800 miles in four days.

The leg rings, or bands, not only prove the speed and distance, but also show the possible life span of a bird in the wild. There is evidence that a curlew can live for thirty years ; gulls and terns for twenty to twenty-five years ; and swallows and swifts up to sixteen years. Conversely, they have shown, too, the enormous mortality rate among migrants ; for example, 63 per cent of our swallows are lost on their travels north and south. These losses can be attributed to weather conditions, and to the wholesale slaughter of migrating wild birds which is practised in several Mediterranean countries, notably Italy.

High winds will, obviously, blow birds off their course ; but fog is an even worse hazard. If the sun or the stars are obliterated by blankets of fog, the migrants are without any means of navigation.

Oddly enough, radar beams also affect birds,

interfering with their chronometer and compass mechanism, and bringing them to earth. This effect has been used in Canada to bring down migrating waterfowl for ringing.

While more than half the travelling swallows die in the course of their journey, they seem less prone to accidents when they are in Britain than martins and swifts.

I have cared for several visiting swifts, which usually stayed only long enough to ride out the gale which had grounded them. These birds, which superficially resemble the swallow tribe, are no relation ; and a closer look shows that they are structurally quite different, designed for an almost totally aerial existence.

The wings are scythe-like and enormous compared with the slim body, while the skull is flat and allows more room for eye-sockets than for brains. As in a nightjar, the bill is tiny but hides a large gape which enables the bird to fly with its mouth wide open to act as a sort of butterfly-net in which to catch aerial plankton—midges, aphids, mayflies and such.

When a young swift leaves the nest for the first time it must pick the right day, for it has no alternative but to fly high and no means of landing on anything except the vertical wall below the nest site, from which it can scramble up under the eaves. This is because, unlike swallows and martins, swifts are unable to perch. In the course of evolution their legs have shortened to mere stumps, covered in coarse furry feathers, and ending in four forward-pointing toes equipped with sharp claws. These feet have a powerful grip which can be extremely painful if the bird happens to fasten them into a soft portion of one's hand, and it is difficult to make them let go.

The commonest swift casualty in my experience was the fledgling that had chosen a windy day for its initial flight, and most of these could be released from the attic window after a few hours when the weather had improved ; but one individual had to stay for several days because of a relentless gale.

On the ground, these birds are like an aircraft with a broken undercarriage. Their wing-span is so enormous in relation to the length of their legs that they are unable to get any impetus with which to launch themselves upwards, and so remain spread-eagled and helpless. They can run up a rough vertical surface but cannot reverse ; and as their whole physical being is concentrated on almost perpetual flight, their care in temporary captivity is extremely difficult.

During the day I found the solution to this difficulty by wearing the young swift like a corsage. It was quite content to remain attached to my clothes while I went about the day's chores ; and after a while I became accustomed to this curious decoration, even to the extent of forgetting it when I answered the door-bell, and several tradesmen may have gone away to sign the pledge in consequence. . . .

As with the wagtails and the martin, a large amount of the time had to be spent catching flies for the swift, and so it was altogether a relief when a fine morning dawned and I carried it for the last time up to the attic window to watch it swoop away across the river and up into the sky.

A swift in its element has all the symmetry and beauty of a well-designed jet aircraft, but on close acquaintance I have found them unattractive, not to say rather creepy. They have a cold reptilian gaze quite unlike the bright-eyed, intelligent glance of most birds, and the vice-grip of their toes and the sudden speed with which they can run up a sleeve and arrive somewhere at the back of one's neck, tend to make the most ardent bird lover uneasy.

Perhaps, of all birds, the passerines that hunt their food by eye and ear are the most attractive, and of these the song-thrush appeals to me most of all. It was, therefore, depressing to find that fledglings of this species were always difficult to rear. I failed over and over again, wasting hours of time trying to persuade a sulky little bird to open its clam-tight bill and take the food it so sorely needed, until, inevitably, it died.

I told juvenile would-be rescuers of young thrushes to leave them where they were, whatever the circumstances, but, every year, one or two would arrive, the victims of cats or traffic. The root of the hand-rearer's problem is the natural disposition of a song-thrush, which is a highly strung creature and subject to fits of unfounded fright. This is well known by British bird fanciers, who are half-way to a first prize if they can stage a tame one at a cage-bird show.

Clearly, I had to find a solution to the problem and, as so often happens, the most unlikely idea succeeded. The usual fledgling, frozen with fright, arrived, but this time I made no attempt to hand-feed it and instead put the bird into a box cage, provided with a stone and a heap of garden snails, the shells cracked with a hammer. I then retired to watch events.

The young thrush squatted glumly on the floor for some time, then the snails caught its eye and I saw a stirring of interest ; its mind was considering these objects which were instinctively familiar, striking a chord somewhere in the brain. Then it moved cautiously towards the heap and gave the nearest snail a tentative dab ; and in doing this must have tasted a morsel, for the penny dropped and the bird was galvanised into furious action.

Bits of shell and horrid bits of snail flew in every direction to stick on the walls and ceiling of the cage, as the fledgling alternately bashed and gobbled its grisly meal. An adult song-thrush is able to eat an entire snail, but the muscular gastropod ' foot ' proved too tough for the young bird, and it contented itself with the softer parts. This meant that a large number of snails were needed, and indeed, a dozen every day was only just enough.

Supplies in my own garden soon ran out and I had to go farther afield, accumulating jam-pots-full as a store to meet the ever increasing demands of my thrush. No-one could look on this baby as a lovesome thing, as it sat on the cage floor amidst a scene of horrible devastation, but it was a great source of pride to me.

The cage reminded one in truth of 'the worst excesses of the French Revolution', and so the bird became known as Madame Defarge, a name that stuck long after both her appearance and habits had improved. But her unpleasant aspect was not really her fault : at the age of eighteen days or so, she was barely ready to leave the nest, and certainly not nearly old enough to feed herself on any kind of food, let alone large and sticky garden snails ; and the result was a face and chest smeared and matted with substances that did not bear contemplation.

After a week I arranged a glass dish of water and persuaded Madame to take a bath, and this she did every day, which enhanced her beauty as layers of dirt were successively removed to be replaced with leopard-spotted plumage on the breast, fading to white underneath ; while the head, back and fast-growing tail became a pastel shade of brown.

The eyes of a thrush are its most beautiful feature : large, liquid and intelligent, and slightly forward-set as it is a hunter. Later, when she learned to eat a less specialised diet, I watched Madame Defarge digging at a grass clump in the aviary ; pausing to listen for the movement of an earthworm within, her head cocked on one side and eyes alight with interest, and then attacking the clump again until her quarry was revealed.

This unorthodox method of rearing produced a splendid adult bird and, surprisingly, one that was quite as tame as any hand-reared fledgling ; and so, at last, I was able to accept orphaned song-thrushes without a feeling of hopelessness and sorrow.

Blackbirds are members of the same family but are different both in character and behaviour, and the young are easily reared. On one occasion I had two from the same nest, the survivors of a raid by an arboreal-minded cat. These two were reared on scrambled egg (which is better than hard-boiled egg for young birds of the smaller species), for the first couple of weeks and then weaned on to Sluisfood, meal-worms and fruit. Both missel-thrushes and black-birds will eat large amounts of fruit (thus, under natural conditions, distributing the seeds in their droppings), taking the berries of hawthorn, mountain ash, elder, ivy and holly, as well as garden soft fruits and blackberries.

The pair of young blackbirds began their education for a wild life by spending the day in an aviary, with their cage hung on the inside wall. Each night they went to bed in the cage, which was then brought indoors. After a month of this it was time for the next stage, and I stood the cage by an open window in the kitchen and allowed them out.

They treated a small area of garden outside the window as if it were an enclosure, returning as before to their cage every evening. Soon the two showed the natural pugnacity of blackbirds, defending their territory against all comers, and even exchanging rude remarks with the jackdaws, Currant and Chestnut —evidently relying on the security of the intervening wire of their aviary, because most small birds give jackdaws and magpies a wide berth, and their young instinctively 'freeze' at the sight of one.

Towards autumn the pair gradually wandered farther afield, with lapses of several days between visits to the kitchen, and finally they left altogether to live their own wild lives.

Their departure was a relief, because they were not good mixers and I had to keep them apart from a young starling, which liked to spend most of its time riding on my shoulder, demanding food and attention with raucous shrieks in my ear. It wanted everything I had, including cigarettes, and would run down my arm to snatch food from my plate at meals.

In order to have some measure of freedom myself, I insisted that the bird spend some of the day in a large cage in the garden ; and, as luck would have it, a family party of starlings elected to visit the bird-table near by. Their endless chatter struck a chord of memory for the young bird and, when it was released, it joined them gladly and was welcomed in return.

It is possible to rear any young bird once a successful method has been evolved with the aid of reference books on bird behaviour, imagination, and trial and error ; the parents are ruthless with weakly nestlings, and these are either trodden underfoot by their stronger brethren or thrown out of the nest altogether. This is a cruel-to-be-kind system, for there is no place for a weakling in the wild.

I have met one occasion when parent birds had evidently been mistakenly soft-hearted. A fledgling rook was brought to me after it had been found tumbling about at the foot of an elm tree in a village garden. At first sight I thought it had been damaged by the fall and, as it was hopelessly maimed, destroyed it at once ; but subsequent examination proved that the unfortunate creature was deformed on hatching— the leg bones were curved in a bow, and the upper mandible of its beak was out of alignment and had grown downwards in a parrot-like hook. Why and how the rooks had reared this poor monster remains a mystery.

CHAPTER EIGHT : THE UGLY DUCKLING

EVERY year a pair of mute swans brought their family down-river from the nest site to the bay : swimming in single file, the cob leading, followed by four or five cygnets, and with the pen acting as rearguard. They came with good reason. The charm of very young cygnets is unique, and in the village there were plenty of people to fall under their spell, searching the larders for stale bread with which to feed the waiting birds.

These habitual daily visits ultimately caused the downfall of the family. A group of youths, bored with the limited possibilities of a surrealist stretch of sand, and abandoned by their charabanc till the evening, found the cygnets alone on the shore while the parent birds foraged in the river. That year five had been hatched, and at the time of the disaster were still clothed in grey fluff and about the size of month-old goslings.

One survived. It was found sprawled on the mud of a dry-dock in a shipyard across the bay, very weak but alive. I never knew the fate of the remainder, but imagine that they took refuge in scattered directions and died in the course of a day or so. The cob and his mate went away.

The survivor arrived at my door in a cat-basket,

its neck protruding through the half-opened lid; black, boot-button eyes glazed with exhaustion and fear. I was prepared for its arrival in the forlorn hope that several members of the family might be found and saved, and so it went straight out to a grass run, provided with a wooden shelter and shallow sink full of water.

Food was an immediate need and I gave it brown bread soaked in milk and fortified with cod-liver oil, and once I was out of range the cygnet began to eat hungrily, sputtering the food in its bill in the same way as a domestic duck. Its short experience of life on the estuary had accustomed it to the company of gulls, and so I introduced two that were in temporary residence at the time into the enclosure, with the idea of providing reassurance by means of familiar objects.

The gulls had the desired effect and the cygnet soon gathered enough courage and energy to investigate the pond. I had littered the shelter with a deep bed of straw and, when the bird had eaten and drunk its fill, I persuaded it with gentle shooing to retire to this bed, where it sank down thankfully.

In the days that followed, it did nothing but eat and rest, and gradually gained weight and confidence; looking on me as the provider of the next meal and not as a terrifying enemy. The dogs had more trouble, but in the end their complete detachment won the day, and as time went on the bird was brave enough to try a pinch or two as they passed.

There is something magical and majestic about a

swan that affects us all ; a heritage from fairy-tales and the early days of solely royal ownership ; of swan-upping and *Swan Lake*. Yet, only half a century ago fattened cygnets were a common sight in London markets, brought there from the last fattening-ground, the Swanpit at Norwich.

The mute swan is supposed to have been introduced into Britain by Richard Cœur de Lion in the twelfth century, and certainly it is traditionally and lawfully regarded as a Bird Royal, protected by ancient laws, which may well represent the first enactments for the purpose of conserving wild-life in this country.

In the reign of Elizabeth I the Royal Swanherd held jurisdiction over the whole of England, and no subject could possess a swan unless he also obtained a licence from the crown. At that time some nine hundred swan marks were recognised, and the bill of each bird was notched so that the ownership of a game (or flock) of swans was clearly shown.

Today only the Queen and the Companies of Dyers and Vintners own swans, which are still rounded up on the Thames every summer in the historic and picturesque ceremony of swan-upping ; while over the rest of the country swans flourish where they will.

Truly wild or semi-tame, they have ceased to be meat for a banquet, and offer nothing but their aesthetic charm, coupled with the magnificence that makes them one of the largest waterfowl and the heaviest flying birds in the world.

Mute swans seldom migrate to and from the British Isles, but in their native Europe wander considerable distances, ranging from Scandinavia to Mongolia. One of the largest European communities is found at Lake Takern in Sweden, where up to a thousand pairs have bred. In Britain about five hundred usually nest at Abbotsbury, while in the extreme north some hundred and fifty pairs have been counted on South Uist. Elsewhere they establish smaller swanneries, depending on the availability of food and suitable nest sites.

Unlike true sea birds, the swan needs fresh water to drink, but this does not prevent it from living on sea lochs or estuaries where it often becomes omnivorous , eating fish, worms, molluscs and garbage, in addition to a normal vegetarian diet of water weeds, grass and other herbage. Birds on salt or brackish water resort to the mouth of a stream several times a day, drinking deeply before returning to forage along the shore.

While living in communities outside the breeding-season, swans pair for life and show great devotion to each other, and to their cygnets, which remain under their care until the following year. Then, as the cob begins his courtship displays in preparation for mating, the unfortunate yearlings are chased with the same ferocity that is doled out to wandering bachelor swans.

These young ones are pathetic in their attempts to return to the fold, coming again and again only to be beaten off with hisses and threats that may turn to actual attack if they persist.   Disillusioned at last, they gradually join groups of other outcasts to form a teen-age flock from which new pairs emerge in the following years.

The pen passively accepts this casting out of her children, and busies herself with finding a site for the new nest.   Once this is selected, she sets to work on building a large mound made from the sticks and weed brought to her by the cob.   The nest may be anything up to five feet in diameter, and about two feet high, with the central cup moulded out by movements of the bird's feet and body in readiness for the clutch of five to a dozen eggs.

Incubation is slow and the pen can be seen enthroned on her monstrous nest for five or six weeks before the eggs hatch.   At this time the cob can be dangerous, and may attack anything that moves near the nest, using his wings and saw-edged bill on a straying cow, a man or a dog—often killing the latter.

As with all animals, the threat posture of a swan is designed to make it appear larger than life.   To this end the wing primaries are erected over the back, almost in the form of a tunnel, while the head is drawn back to touch these arched feathers, and the bird ceases to be a gentle Narcissus and becomes instead a hell-bent battleship.

The cygnets take to the water, like ducklings, soon after hatching, but it is five months before they are able to fly, for although nidifugous chicks, they are more dependent on their parents than most.   My poor cygnet was an example of this dependence, which, as it became tame, was transferred to its new human family.

Working out a system of management for a small cygnet had its problems, and I made several mistakes before I learned how to look after the bird properly. The first was forgivable, as it was based on experience with ducklings and goslings, which thrive on chicken-mash and milk, with the addition of soft green stuff such as chickweed and lettuce.   But cygnets are different.

Swans, with the aid of their long necks, take most of their food underwater ; biting off weeds, sieving the adhering mud and other inedible items in the bill, and siphoning the debris out through the nostrils by releasing a stream of air-bubbles.

The cygnet ate mash and milk in this way, and very soon the nostrils were blocked with caked meal, causing it distress.   I sat the bird on my knee and cleared both passages with a match-stick wrapped in cotton-wool, blowing down each hole to remove the last particles.   This operation was very easy because the bird appeared to understand what I was doing, and showed no resentment.   To complete the job, I then carried it down to the shore when the tide was in and the water calm, and after fitting a makeshift harness and lead, allowed it to swim in the shallows, wading in its wake.

At first the bathe was a great success.   We swam and waded in circles, the cygnet plunging its head below the surface to gubble sand on the bottom, sending up streams of bubbles through the cleared nostrils ; but, after a few minutes, it seemed to remember where it was and what had happened when it was last on the estuary—the chasing and the volley of stones and tin cans—and panic set in.

I carried the frightened bird back to the garden, and it was some time before it recovered. We experimented once more with a bathe a few days later, but the result was the same, and so these outings had to be abandoned.

The diet problem was solved by feeding brown bread-and-milk as a staple, with cut grass and bunches of chickweed provided, floating in the sink bath. The food dish was set beside the sink so that the cygnet could alternately eat and rinse its bill, and sandwich the green stuff between beakfuls of bread and milk. This system suited it well, and there was no more trouble with the nostrils, and its droppings were firm and goose-like.

My next error was to forget what I knew about the hazards of rearing domestic waterfowl without the benefit of their parents' preen-oil. A duckling, still wearing fluffy down-feathers, is not able to waterproof its own plumage from the uropygial gland, but obtains enough oil for the purpose from its mother's body while she is brooding it. Consequently, ducklings or goslings raised in a brooder or by a farmyard hen are at the mercy of rainstorms, and even subject to fatal chilling if they are allowed to swim for any length of time.

The cygnet had no instinctive idea of taking shelter in a man-made wooden hut, and so it sat out in a torrential downpour which soaked its down-feathers to the skin. I dried it indoors and gave it a warm meal, but the damage was done ; next day its pleasant piping voice had altered to a hoarse croak and the food was left untouched.

I telephoned the vet for advice, and was told that a bottle would be made up for me to collect. The bottle contained a bright pink, sticky fluid, and was labelled, ' Medicine for Cygnet, 1 teaspoonful 3 times a day '.

In the course of the preceding weeks the cygnet had grown quite considerably, and if it was necessary to carry the bird, I had to hold its body under one arm with the neck held in the other hand for support and control, while its large flat feet pedalled wildly out behind. Clearly it hated to be handled, like all but the tamest birds, and so I drove it when a move from here to there was required. But now I had to pour a nasty-tasting liquid down its throat three times a day, and the prospect was not a happy one.

But I need not have worried. Without any previous experience of swan management, it was easy to forget the innate intelligence of these birds, and I was surprised at the philosophic way in which the cygnet accepted its medicine. Morning, noon and night, I knelt over it as it sat in its pen, the bottle and teaspoon beside us, prized open its bill and poured in the dose ; carefully holding the head level to avoid choking and giving the medicine a drip at a time for the same reason.

Next morning, though still hoarse, the bird was eating and in a few days it was back to normal ; but, to make sure, the dosing was kept up for a week. Certainly, without it my ownership of a swan would have been a short-lived affair.

By October the hitherto ugly duckling had begun to show promise of the swan to come. It was then clothed in brown feathers, which had grown over the down, and now a patch or two of white began to appear amongst the dark plumage ; and the bird compared in size with an average domestic goose.

It is difficult to determine the sex of a swan until it is adult and the black knob at the base of the bill shows by its size whether the bird is a cob or pen. Cygnets have a greyish bill and only a vestigial black knob, but this begins to swell after about eight months, as the bill gradually turns to the familiar orange colour of a full-grown swan. The metamorphosis from awkward babyhood to adult splendour is slow and almost imperceptible, but at the age of twelve months it is complete, although another four years may elapse before the bird will mate.

As my cygnet was, as yet, too young to show any outward clues to its sex, I had to make a guess from its behaviour. I had found that the wooden hut, which had served as a shelter when the bird was small, was soon outgrown, as swans like to stand up and stretch their necks, and the low roof of this hut meant that every time the cygnet stretched, its head struck the ceiling. I had to shut it in at night for fear of foxes, and so a roomy shed was cleared out and bedded with straw, and every evening we walked there, the bird turning in at the right door and settling itself comfortably on the straw nest. As it settled, it picked up lengths of straw and arranged them carefully, at the same time shuffling with its feet and body to form a cup-shaped centre. I took this behaviour as fairly certain proof that I owned a pen.

Clearly, she needed a name and it must be a magnificent one. Gloria was the best I could think of, and it seemed to suit her because in a short time she would answer to it—either actively by coming for her food, or vocally from a distance in reply to idiotic inquiries about her health and well-being.

'Mute' swan is a curiously inept description of such a talkative species. When Gloria had outgrown her juvenile piping voice, she acquired a series of notes, most of which were addressed to us as conversation, varying from grunts, honks and trumpeting to a gentle whistle; while strangers were greeted with fierce hissing to hide the fact that she is an extremely timid bird.

As I could provide only a small pond, Gloria had to spend an unnatural amount of time on land, and as she grew and her weight touched the twenty-pound mark, with the probability that she would ultimately weigh twice as much, I wondered if she might develop

leg weakness. Fortunately, however, she adapted herself and the legs became unusually sturdy with use
and with the help of a rich diet.

In the course of time she evolved a pattern to her
day ; dividing the time between grazing on the lawn,
and neatly folded repose, the neck resting on her
mantle and head tucked among the primaries, but
with one dark eye watching everything that went on
about her. In this position she became coracle-
shaped and would be buoyant and just as comfortable
afloat, for even her legs were tucked away in the
plumage of her thighs.

I have found that all sea birds take up this attitude
when they are resting. The legs are withdrawn largely
for reasons of warmth, but also for safety while the
bird is relaxed, because a large fish would not be
above taking a snap at the leg of an aquatic bird,
and a number of sea birds do, in fact, lose a limb in
this way—particularly the black-headed gull with its
attractive red legs.

The character and intelligence of individuals and
species as a whole is more interesting to me than
watching them through binoculars, though I appreciate
that the scientific bird-watcher achieves more than I
do. It was, therefore, fascinating to be able to know
a swan personally and compare her I.Q. with those of
a number of other visiting birds, great and small.

I have reached the conclusion that, within her
physical limitations, Gloria's intelligence compares
favourably with that of an average dog. She is

able to learn from a single experience, subsequently using the information to her advantage ; while in an unprecedented situation she will take the most sensible course.

Perhaps the most outstanding ability is her understanding of doors. If she is hungry or lonely Gloria comes in search of me in the house ; one hears a distant heavy tread and bass grunts, and then a head peers through the doorway, the voice changing to whistles of recognition. Should the back door be closed, she will plod round to the front and come in at the hall door, making her way down two passages to the kitchen, after a glance in at the sitting-room to find it empty.

Among waterfowl, only a razorbill learned about doors to the same extent. This bird was an oil victim that made a prolonged stay due to wet-feather, and so became known as Bill. Bill spent most of his time in the garden, free to wander where he would, but at regular intervals pattered indoors for food, as he had to be hand-fed. In windy weather the door would be shut, but that did not deter this wild bird which had spent its whole life at sea, and he would stand in the yard croaking with a sound like an elderly grandfather clock whirring towards striking the hour, impatiently waiting for someone to open the door. As soon as someone did, he hurried past into the kitchen to stand by the 'fridge, where he patently knew his fish was kept.

It is almost incredible that a bird should be able

to appreciate the mechanics of a house, so that it knows that a call outside an apparently blank wall will be answered by an invisible human being beyond it, resulting in a hole appearing in the wall through which it can enter.

But the razorbill's understanding was limited to a known route, whereas Gloria will find her way in strange surroundings and has other interests besides food. Her sense of intelligent curiosity is much the same as that shown by Orry and by Phillip, the crow, but it is not possible to assess their comparative abilities together because she is pinioned, while they had the advantage of flight.

The time it takes various smaller species to understand how to use feeding-devices provides a yardstick to measure their intellect. In this case, house-sparrows head the class, with the goldfinch and greenfinch as runners-up. In a mixed aviary containing these species and a linnet, the first three learned to use a seed-hopper of fairly complicated design within a matter of minutes, but the linnet had to be fed from a dish for several months before the fact that the hopper offered food dawned on him.

Among insectivores, a spotted flycatcher and a wren reached a high plane, accepting temporary captivity, and eating manufactured food from a dish without any introduction by means of live food. The same applied to a seed-eating yellow-hammer. She arrived as a stunned road casualty, due for only a brief stay before being returned to her territory, but during that twenty-four-hour rest she learned to use both a hopper and a water fountain as if to the manner born.

I am irritated by people who support the theory that the behaviour of animals is motivated entirely by responses to stimuli and similar claptrap. Birds and mammals live in a different dimension from human beings, and we can never look out through the window of their eyes to see the minutiae of the world in which they live.

CHAPTER NINE : ATTIC MEWS

THE common buzzard, like the common gull, is not so common as its name implies. Since the introduction of myxomatosis to Britain and the consequent decimation of the rabbit population, the number of buzzards has decreased enormously, for these birds were slow to adapt themselves to a new way of life, and in the process a great many died of starvation.

At this time a workman from the village bicycled every day to the local town, on each trip passing a solitary buzzard perched on the same fence post. One morning he stopped to throw down a ham sandwich from his lunch-box, and the bird instantly jumped to the ground and ate this strange meal. And so a daily ritual began, and soon the buzzard would lean forward from its perch to take the sandwich out of his gloved hand, eating the bread and salt meat ravenously ; until a day when it was missing from its post and was not seen again.

That same year I saw another buzzard dodging the traffic to tear pieces from a dead cat which had been killed by a car ; and local farmers were shooting the hawks that plucked up enough courage to raid poultry yards. These birds must have been desperate indeed, because a buzzard, for all its eagle-like appearance, is a sheep in wolf's clothing, and for this reason has never been used for falconry.

Then, with the arrival of another summer, a resurgence seemed to occur ; the survivors made a nucleus for a new buzzard population, able to scrape a living in constant competition with owls and other birds of prey, weasels, stoats and foxes, all of whom were now eating fledgling birds, small rodents, beetles, reptiles and frogs, and even vegetable matter, in order to live.

A few dead buzzards were still found now and again, and when the contents of their stomachs were examined, they were shown to contain little more than earthworms and herbage, and clearly, the birds had died from the related causes of digestive disturbance due to a starvation diet.

Several species of birds disgorge pellets as a regular part of their digestive processes ; for instance, ravens and curlews both do it ; and the production of pellets is universal amongst birds of prey, which become ill if there is insufficient roughage in their food to make material for these regurgitated parcels.

The ground below the favourite perch of an owl or a hawk will provide a number of specimen pellets, and it is always interesting to examine these and discover the type of food the bird has taken. A typical owl pellet is cigar-shaped, the outer covering made from the skins of mice, and packed inside with small bones, beetle wings and other spiky debris. How the stomach arranges each pellet with a smooth casing

6

over the hard materials is a minor wonder of nature, allowing the bird to eat totally indigestible portions of food without any danger to the delicate membranes of its interior.

The only disadvantage of this system is that the digestion of a carnivorous bird is entirely dependent on its proper functioning, and if pellets are not ejected every day illness will follow.

In the course of a series of talks which I gave to groups of women's clubs, I found that the inclusion of a question-time produced items of much greater interest than my own notes ; and I was amazed at the amount of time and trouble some of these ladies had devoted to a stray fledgling or a wounded bird of one sort or another.

Many had made the usual mistakes of over-feeding and over-handling their patients ; one had poured lemonade down the throat of an injured kittiwake, which proceeded to choke to death ; another had reared and released a nestful of swallows, without apparently realising that there was anything remarkable about this feat ; and several, over the years, had attempted to bring up a baby owl, all without success. (The explanation of this was an owl killed with kindness. Like the adult, the young bird of prey must have roughage in its food to survive.)

With the local buzzard population in such a precarious state, it was inevitable that, sooner or later, I would have one as a patient. In due course the telephone rang one evening ; a woman living in a neighbouring village had come home to find her outer porch door closed, and on the mat inside was lying a very sick buzzard. It was supposed that some school-children had brought it, knowing that she was fond of birds, and when they got no answer at the door, left it on the mat.

When I arrived the bird had been transferred to a cardboard box, lined with hay, where it lay half on its side, wicked talons and open bill showing a pathetic attempt at ferocity, for the poor creature was too weak to move. As I watched, its eyes closed and I thought it would probably be dead by the morning, but, even so, it was worth having a shot at reviving it.

That night I had no food in the house suitable for a starving buzzard, and it had to make do with what there was. I collected together some small pieces of cooked mutton cut from the Sunday joint, a halibut-oil capsule, a tablet of concentrated yeast (in case the bird was suffering from the first signs of insecticide poisoning), a little creamy milk and three drops of gin in a teaspoon.

Slowly and gently I persuaded this strange meal down the gullet of the prostrate buzzard, and then carried it, in its box, up to an empty attic room. I had little hope of seeing it alive next day, but set a mouse-trap in the wood-shed all the same.

At first light I went upstairs, holding a dead mouse by the tail, and quietly opened the attic door. The buzzard was perched on the edge of her box, her great eyes widening with fear at the sight of me, but when I skated the mouse across the floor a taloned foot flashed out to seize it. I left her with it, and went downstairs to set about laying in a stock of rabbit meat, liver and chickens' heads.

An obliging poulterer provided rabbit joints and a head, which I gave to the bird in a flat glass dish. She could not resist this meal of a lifetime and started in on it while I stood near, watching as she grabbed each piece in her talons and tore it in bits with her powerful bill. On this visit I found a small pellet which she had ejected, and when this was examined under a magnifying-glass I found that it consisted of a bundle of fibrous grass roots, the skins of three ' woolly-bear ' caterpillars and one leather-jacket, and the wing cases of a small beetle. It was no wonder that the bird had collapsed !

The buzzard is a big bird, considerably larger than a peregrine falcon, with a normal weight of about two and a half pounds. My bird weighed little more than twelve ounces when she arrived. Her sex was obvious from her size, as, in birds of prey, the female of the species is always larger than the male, and this one was very large indeed ; in fact, she was nearly twice the size of a barn owl.

A hawk of these dimensions might have been awe-inspiring, and I was careful when it was necessary to handle her, but she was not in the least ferocious ; only frightened and weak. The edge of a cardboard box was no place for such a bird to sit, and so, with gloved hands, I moved her to a wooden block in a corner of the room and covered the surrounding floor area with newspapers.

The toes of hawks are spread and, for this reason, they are more comfortable perched on a post than on a horizontal branch. The legs and feet are canary-yellow in colour ; the long talons a polished black, and these are the real weapons, rather than the dangerous-looking hooked bill, because they are capable of an iron grip which will pierce a human hand without any effort.

Gauntlet gloves are, therefore, a ' must ' for a handler of birds of prey as, however tame a hawk or an owl may be, the first sign of tension is shown by a contraction of the claws, and I remember vividly seeing the hand of a small boy after his pet owl had gripped it, leaving him with a stigma for life.

The buzzard appeared more at ease once she was settled on her block, and I left her alone most of the time so that she could relax and make the best use of the food which was all that was needed for recovery. A greater part of the day was spent in somnolent contemplation, but sometimes when I came in she would be crouched over a chunk of meat, and a large dish of water and its surroundings proved that she had bathed rather thoroughly.

Concentrated nourishment was an obvious neces-sity, and so, at first, half her daily ration was made up of chicken and rabbit livers, daubed with moulted feathers collected from the cages of my other visitors, which provided material for her pellets. These began to take on the normal appearance of miniature cigars, tightly packed with rabbit fur, feathers and small skull bones that she had torn from the unskinned heads.

For the first week she was unable to fly, and only ventured from her block for food and water, but then I moved her to an imitation post, set in the middle of the room with a view of the window, and on my next visit I found her standing on the sill looking out through the panes, which she evidently realised were barriers.

By that time, I could persuade her to perch on my fist by pressing gently behind her legs with a gloved hand, forcing her to step backwards in order to keep her balance. This led to the next stage : fitting a set of jesses.

A jess is a short leather strap, traditionally made from dog skin, slit lengthways at either end so that it will loop through itself. One end of a jess is attached to each of the hawk's legs and they are joined at a swivel, to which a further strap is fastened and held in the falconer's hand. Bells are also worn by hunting-hawks so that they can be heard if they are lost out of sight.

I acquired a set of jesses in Ireland, and have found them useful in controlling various kinds of large perching-birds, and particularly in the case of the buzzard, who accepted them calmly, enabling me to carry her downstairs to spend days out in an aviary. While she was out of doors, I had to arrange

screens so that she was invisible to the other cage
and aviary birds, who might have become hysterical
with fright, or with a desire to mob this huge hawk
that had invaded their territory.

Mobbing is an extraordinary example of social
behaviour in birds, and is not confined to those species
that congregate in flocks. Blackbirds, which are
solitary and bad-tempered outside the breeding-season
and occupy fiercely defended territories when they
are nesting, will gather together and mob a cat
that is stalking a fledgling belonging to one of the
pairs engaged in the attack. I have seen a cat
running for its life, pursued by ' dive-bombing '
swallows ; and, on several occasions, an owl trying
to evade the attacks of a mixed flock of finches.

These hysterically courageous attacks are released
by an alarm call from an individual or because all the
birds can see the source of danger, and they join in a
mass attack which unnerves a predator that would
normally kill any one of their number if it were alone.

In the course of a few weeks the buzzard began to
gain condition, her breast became plump and there
was a marked difference in the weight of the bird as
she perched on my fist. She began to fly about the
attic and to spend a lot of time gazing out of the
window, and I realised that she was ready to leave.

This moment arrives with all the patients that
make a full recovery. They seem to accept captivity
as a means to an end, taking advantage of the chance
to eat and rest in security until they feel fit to live

in the wild once more ; then their behaviour changes, and for the first time they react to a cage or aviary as to a prison, and the time has come for them to go.

The actual release presents a number of problems. The question of territories is the most difficult, because, while birds which live in flocks, such as finches and starlings, can join a crowd of their kind, species that are solitary outside the breeding-season and maintain strict territories whether they are nesting or not, will attack a wandering stranger and attempt to kill it.

This means that, in the case of robins, thrushes and other resident species maintaining a territory, the only time when a newcomer has any hope of acceptance is in the late summer when the year's crop of young birds are on the move and the residents expect strangers in their midst.

Fortunately, a territory is not lost if the owner can be returned to it within a week or so, but it takes fine judgement to decide that a bird is fit to find its own living after such a short period of convalescence, how-ever important it may be to keep its territory. It is no kindness to patch up an injured bird and then release it to die of starvation.

Just as birds with a future in the wild show by their behaviour when they are fit for release, those that must remain in captivity seem to accept the inevitable and settle down remarkably well. This is partly due to two types of treatment. When a bird arrives, I assess its prospects as best I can, and then arrange its management to suit the case. The short-term patient is not tamed more than is necessary or unavoidable, whereas the bird that must remain in an aviary is talked to and persuaded to trust the human being it recognises.

Complete tameness with anyone takes much longer to achieve in a bird that has been adult in the wild, but, though this might appear obvious, it is often difficult to explain to visitors who ask to see my birds.

An odd aspect of human behaviour is that people with normal sight become suddenly myopic when they are faced with an animal in a cage, and seem incapable of looking at it without pressing their faces to the bars. A pet budgerigar is able to stand this kind of treatment, but it is terrifying for a former wild bird, because this sort of fixed stare is exactly like the action of a predator on the point of attack.

At the same time, there is considerable propaganda value in showing the public what happens to birds : that driving a car through a flock feeding on the road will result in maiming such as this or this ; protecting garden seeds with fine cotton thread or rotting nets will cause a broken wing or leg ; so will an array of overhead wires unless marked with corks ; and, even, pouring engine sump-oil down a main drain can pollute the plumage of waterfowl on a river miles away.

There was a keen demand for a view of the buzzard, and she was one of the few birds who could survive an inspection without flinching. She sat on her block, great yellow eyes returning the inevitable human stare with a total lack of interest.

I decided to release her locally, as there was a solitary buzzard in a coppice on the hill behind the village, and I thought from its size that it was probably a male. She sailed out of her attic window, huge wings flapping, and swooped away up the hill in the planned direction ; in the succeeding weeks a pair were seen in the trees, and they could be heard mewing to each other as they planed in the sky, their eyes focused on the fields below, waiting for a small movement that might betray a mouse or a beetle.

There was no certainty about her prospects of survival, but I hoped that a large area untenanted by other birds of prey might be enough to support this pair.

She was not the first bird of prey to be accommodated in the attic room. A tragic and brief visit was made by a barn owl, suffering from a bullet wound in the shoulder. Almost certainly, this had been inflicted by a trigger-happy youth, armed with a ·22 rifle and presented with a sitting target.

As the law stands today, any child can obtain a gun licence if it is able to sign its own name. This means that a child of only eight could carry a lethal weapon, capable of killing or injuring other children and adults, besides farm stock and wild-life. It seems almost incredible that the law should be so carefree about allowing children to carry firearms, when most continental countries only issue licences at the discretion of the police to persons over the age of eighteen, often requiring a proficiency and safety test as well.

The potential power of a shotgun to cause appalling injury is only apparent at close range. I remember shooting a large rat with a twelve-bore from a distance of about six feet ; the animal was, literally, blown to pieces. It is easy to imagine the impact in terms of wounding on a small child.

A ·22 rifle has a much greater range, and a slug from it is just as deadly if it finds a vital spot ; yet every year doting parents give children guns, and only rarely add any instructions about safety precautions or marksmanship.

I have met quite a number of people who thought that the Bird Protection Act covers all wild birds, apart from preserved game, and I have not disillusioned them ; although, in fact, several species remain unprotected, but the barn owl is not one of these.

Any injured bird is a sad sight but, of all, perhaps a creature as beautiful and harmless (not to say valuable) as an owl is the most pathetic. It is a bird of innate dignity and great charm, and it was a welcome resident on the farms of our rude and uncivilised ancestors, who built owl holes in their barns to attract a pair of these predators which, in return, checked the rodent population with much greater efficiency than any amount of poisoned bait.

Nowadays, barn owls are rarer, largely because they have eaten rats and mice containing poison, or insects polluted with insecticide.

A cornered owl has one last line of defence, its talons ; and to use these effectively the bird throws itself over on its back. The injured owl persisted in doing this and so I decided to leave it quiet, with a supply of meat and water, to give the metabolism a chance to deal with the wound if this was possible. I hoped that the slug had merely ploughed a furrow through the flesh but, when the bird died some twenty-four hours later, a close examination showed that it had entered the body cavity, causing an internal haemorrhage which could only end in death.

It is difficult not to become unreasonably angry in the face of this kind of vandalism, but the real blame lies in our educational system which lags far behind that of most of western Europe in its attitude to wild-life conservation. Scandinavians are even able to fix nest-boxes in the trees of their public parks, attracting large numbers of wild birds which will remain unmolested. How long such a scheme would last in Britain is not a question for conjecture !

But with the increase in the number and quality of television nature programmes, a new attitude towards wild-life is gradually emerging as people realise that naturalists are not necessarily a band of rather loopy bug-hunters. Not long ago I was subjected to a lecture on the life history of the ant that would have done justice to Fabre himself, but the lecturer was a nine-year-old boy from a secondary school and the source of his knowledge was the ' telly '.

CHAPTER TEN : UNACCUSTOMED AS I AM . . .

ONCE it is known in a country village that you are interested in wild-life, it is taken for granted that your knowledge embraces the care in sickness and in health of the entire animal kingdom. In the course of a day I have been asked to determine the sexes of a boxful of white mice, remove a chop bone wedged across the upper jaw of a by no means co-operative terrier, and retrieve an injured herring gull lying about thirty yards from the shore in a wintry sea.

Such a reputation has its disadvantages, and yet is made worth while by the incidents of humour and pathos which add spice to the absorbing day-by-day work of caring for birds. But a possible vision of myself in the role of a modern Androcles was rudely shattered by a small girl at the door asking for ' the animal-woman ' ; a part at once bereft of romance and endowed with a jungly character reminiscent of a yeti or the lower reaches of the Hollywood film industry.

One year, when the pendulum of popular interest had swung back to the permanent plight of sea birds on oil-polluted waters, I was invited to take part in a B.B.C. television programme, bringing the very tame guillemot, Gilly, with me.

We travelled by train, the bird in a hay-lined cat-basket, alone in the compartment except for an elderly woman who slept peacefully until, as we neared Bristol, Gilly stood up to look out of her basket, which was open on the seat beside me, and voiced a whooping remark which sounded like a fog-bound steamer.

The woman opened her eyes with a start, glanced at me and at what appeared to be a small penguin in a basket, and then averted her gaze to the window.

An hotel had been arranged in advance, but I arrived on its doorstep to be confronted with a large notice forbidding pets. However, I succeeded in smuggling the basket into my room and, with the door locked, gave Gilly a bathe in the wash-hand basin. We had brought with us a supply of sprats in a plastic container, and the combined warmth of the train and the central-heating system of the hotel had not added to their freshness. In consequence, I spent a restless night and checked out early next morning.

The hours that followed were spent in rehearsals, punctuated by coffee-breaks in the canteen ; while Gilly rested in my dressing-room, conserving herself for the actual broadcast. When the hour approached and my heart was well on its way down to my shoes, I brought her into the studio. She perched contentedly on a table, preening and exercising her wings, entirely undaunted by the batteries of cameras and lights, a microphone swinging from a sort of derrick above our heads and, worst of all, the monitor sets that show you yourself.

I enjoyed the experience in retrospect that time, and genuinely on the next occasion ; but nobody inquired about my feelings and, instead, I was asked a hundred times in the following days if the poor bird had been terrified.

Even a brief appearance on television can spark off invitations to speak to live audiences, and before long I found myself alone on platforms, hoarse-voiced and holding my notes down on the table to prevent them from rattling ; until people laughed when I meant them to (may Heaven reward them !) and I lost myself in the pleasure of talking on a pet subject to an audience who proved that they listened by asking a host of questions.

The most regular questions from any audience were connected with attracting and feeding garden birds ; constructing bird-tables and nest-boxes, the kind of food to provide for various species, and the most useful trees and shrubs to give cover, and food in the form of berries.

The provision of food, water and safe nesting-sites will soon double the number of birds in a residential area, while five times as many will occupy a woodland sanctuary. But before embarking on the establishment of a sanctuary, however small, it is important to consider the future. If it is likely that the house and garden will change hands in a foreseeable time, it is not a good idea to tame wild birds which may

ultimately suffer for it at the hands of strangers—
newcomers who own unruly children, dogs or cats.

A bird-table alone, set up a little distance from
the house, will not persuade birds to lose their natural
watchfulness, but may save their lives in a hard
winter. A serviceable table can be made for about
five shillings from a six-foot post (this allows for
eighteen inches or two feet to be driven into the
ground), surmounted by a board—preferably roofed
to protect the food from bad weather. A thatched
effect can be obtained by tacking on to the roof strips
of the straw mats used for packing wine bottles.

Less enthusiastic carpenters may prefer a joiner-
made table ; but whatever the choice, the result must
be a cafeteria for birds and not a sports arena for
the neighbours' cats.

A horizontal bar, arranged to project at either side
of the table, is a useful addition from which coconuts
and fat can be suspended to encourage the more agile
small birds, like tits and nuthatches, who are otherwise ousted by sparrows and starlings.

Starlings can be a great nuisance at a bird-table,
arriving like a swarm of locusts to clear the food in a
few minutes. The poor creatures are just as hungry
as the more interesting species, but they can eat a
rougher omnivorous diet of table scraps given separ-
ately, and the bird-table can be caged in with wire-
netting to protect the specialised foods. Blue, marsh
and coal tits can pop through three-quarter-inch-mesh
netting, but to cater for great tits and other small

garden birds the mesh, or bars, will have to be larger.

To benefit a wide range of species, the ideal table should consist of a central cage, fitted with a service door, and an outer veranda to provide a feeding-place for medium-sized birds such as thrushes and black-birds and, of course, the starlings.

Before discussing foods, it may be as well to settle the perennial argument about the provision of food on a bird-table during the spring and summer. Fat, bread and coconuts must not be given after the middle of March. These foods are completely unsuitable for baby birds and will cause their deaths.

Winter feeding can begin during the latter half of September. Of all foods for wild birds, fat is the most popular and the most valuable during hard weather. It is a strange tradition that allies drifts of snow and jolly robins as the epitome of Christmas. Winter, at its mildest, is a hazardous time for birds, whose metabolic rates demand constant nourishment. Fat provides this in a quickly assimilated form.

In addition, seeds, nuts, fruit, bread and meal-worms are welcomed, and perhaps the most labour-saving method of providing this range of foods is to combine them in a bird-pudding. Recipes can vary with materials available, but this I offer as a guide :

2–3 lb. raw suet
$\frac{1}{2}$ lb. mixed dried fruit
1 small stale loaf
4 oz. shelled peanuts
1 pkt. dried insects (obtained at pet store)

Fry the suet slowly to extract as much fat as possible, and then, while it is still hot, pour it into a basin containing the fruit, crumbled bread and other ingredients. Mix thoroughly, and allow it to stand until set hard, when it can be turned out on to the bird-table.

Halved coconuts will provide tits with exercise as well as food, and when the shells are emptied they can be refilled with rendered fat or bird-pudding. Whole peanuts strung on wire or string, but not on cotton thread, are equally good ; and odd bits of raw and cooked fat, bread crusts and such, can be impaled on a short length of pliable wire or a skewer in the same way as kebabs, with the skewer fixed to a horizontal bar by a screw hook, and the food pre-vented from slipping down by stopping the lower end with a cork, or by turning the wire with a pair of pliers.

Seeds, either finch mixture or a mixture of wild seeds, can be bought at corn merchants and pet stores, and these may be given throughout the year. So can dried or spoiled fresh fruit, and meal-worms and maggots. Somehow word goes round that live foods are on the menu, and many hitherto unseen species may arrive for lunch, including the woodpeckers.

Once or twice in a decade a winter invasion of redwings will occur ; the birds flocking in vast numbers, particularly in very bad weather, and starving to death in their hundreds. Their shyness prevents them from venturing near a bird-table, and they will not eat fat or bread, and all this is naturally distressing for a householder who is helpless to save the miserable creatures huddling in every corner of the garden. The answer is boiled potatoes and any kind of spoiled fresh fruit, which should be scattered under the bushes where the birds are hiding. They will eat this food and find enough nourishment in it to give them strength to continue their journey southwards.

Water is needed, and in generous quantities, when the birds' natural supplies are frozen over. In very cold weather, when water will freeze in a few minutes, it is best to refill the bird-bath at regular times during the day. The birds will soon learn the routine and their own chronometers will tell them when to expect a drink.

While most people feed wild birds in one way or another, by putting crumbs on a window-sill or maintaining elaborate bird-tables, comparatively few put up nest-boxes for the breeding-season ; yet there are a wide range of designs to suit all kinds of garden birds, and they provide a source of great interest and pleasure.

A typical box for small birds, like tits, is about six inches square and ten inches high at the back, sloping to a seven-inch front, in which a hole, of between one and a quarter and two inches in diameter, is drilled a third of the way up. A door, for inspection and cleaning, is fitted either in one side or by hinging the roof. Otherwise, the only essentials are that the boxes must be proof against wind, rain and predators, and sited to face east or north to avoid direct sunlight and driving rain.

Some boxes offered for sale in shops are fitted with a perch below the pop-hole, and these should not be used, as the perch is an invitation to exploring magpies and squirrels; but birds like flycatchers are more likely to nest in a box if there is a clear flight-way to it and a handy branch near by.

The use of natural bark to decorate a box may please the human eye, but a bird is quite content with an exterior of plain timber, and this is better because it is possible to clean the box inside and out at the end of the year, removing both dirt and minute parasites which would otherwise remain to harm the next brood.

Whenever possible, nest-boxes should be in place before Christmas, when many resident species are already prospecting for sites. The height at which they are hung is not very important, if potential robbers are kept in mind. Clearly, children, cats and rats will find a low nest the easiest to get at, whereas a squirrel or a magpie will go for the ones hung above twelve feet high—although I maintain that the last two are nothing like as black as they are painted. If any form of interference is unlikely, the boxes can be attached to trees, walls and pergola posts, at eye level, or lower, with the advantage that they will then be ignored by sparrows and starlings but readily occupied by other small passerines.

Arranging a garden to encourage wild birds is largely a matter of planting trees and shrubs which offer cover for nest sites, or edible berries. Some plants will provide both.

Obvious choices are holly, hawthorn, elder and mountain ash, privet and cotoneaster ; the latter may bring a flock of waxwings to a garden in south and south-eastern England, as these birds find cotoneaster berries irresistible. A plot of fallow ground where dandelions and thistles are allowed to run wild will attract goldfinches, and if teasel seed is sown here whole flocks of finches are likely to arrive.

In a larger area than the average garden, a few pine and fir trees can be planted for the benefit of goldcrests and siskins, and a thicket of any kind, from hawthorn to bamboo, will soon contain a new population of birds.

These few suggestions by no means exhaust the possibilities of a garden bird-sanctuary ; experience and imagination will find several more ideas to increase both the number and the species that can be attracted by feeding- and nesting-devices.

I must finally mention a related idea : the attraction of butterflies to the flower garden. Two shrubs, both hardy and rapid-growing, will have the most remarkable effect. These are hyssop and buddleia, which produce a nectar liked by red admirals, tortoise-shells, fritillaries and several other large and brightly coloured species.

An increase in the population of wild birds in a

garden will inevitably reduce the possibilities for serious horticulture, and I appreciate that most people will not sacrifice their gardens for the purpose of establishing a large-scale sanctuary. But they can, and should, take steps to preserve the birds that are already in residence ; realising that soft-billed birds eat at least their own weight in harmful insects every day, and the finches that may do minor damage to a fruit crop spend most of the year eating weed seeds.

The thoughtless abandon with which chemicals are thrown about in our countryside is really frightening but, at last, it does seem that various authorities are taking stock of the dangers inherent in this system of scientific agriculture ; looking to a future desert land, bare of wild-life, of bees, honey and fruit.

In 1958 the United States Fish and Wildlife Service stated that they estimated some thirty-five million pounds of arsenic salts and a hundred and thirty million pounds of chlorinated insecticides were distributed over the agricultural and forest lands of their country during the year 1957.

Chlorinated insecticides include DDT, heptachlor and dieldrin, and of these the last is the most deadly. The United States Department of Agriculture has recommended its use at the rate of between two and four pounds to the acre ; yet, tests made by the California Department of Fish and Game have shown that only one and a half pounds of dieldrin have sufficient toxicity to kill about four million game chicks, not to mention all the dogs, cats, domestic fowls, and wild birds, mammals and reptiles, which are unfortunate enough to become contaminated. Moreover, these poisons will persist in soil for several years, and for lesser periods in water.

Further tests have proved that birds in the second generation of exposure to insecticides in their diet invariably become incapable of reproduction, and it seems possible that there may be a similar cumulative effect on mammals, including the species *homo sapiens*.

It is clear that these chemicals are quite as dangerous as radioactive fall-out if they are used indiscriminately, and Britain faces an appalling prospect if she follows the American lead into an age of chemical agriculture that will leave no place for our heritage of wild-life.

The ordinary gardener, least of all, has no need of dieldrin, although it is freely recommended by horti-culturists without any warnings against its dangers. The age-old natural insecticide, pyrethrum, will deal with pest insects missed by the birds without harming other creatures ; and there is a wide range of selective weed-killers which are non-poisonous ; apart from flame-guns, which destroy weeds and insects but leave the garden safe for working bees.

A fruit-grower is usually waging an endless war against all birds, and the bullfinch in particular. I do nothing to distract birds from the blossom or buds, in the firm belief that they are doing more good than harm. Fruit which grows in clusters needs thinning for its proper development, and if the tree has been thoroughly investigated by birds it is unlikely that insects will be able to establish themselves.

But if the grower must do something to discourage the birds, trees and bushes can be sprayed with a solution made with quassia chips, which can be obtained from a chemist. The quassia is a South American tree and the chips, made from its bark and wood, are horribly bitter and unpalatable but quite harmless to all animals.

Apart from quassia, there are numerous methods of protecting crops without endangering wild-life. As an example, there is no need to kill that nice little creature, the mole, when it invades a lawn. The biennial plant, *Euphorbia lathyrus*, which grows wild in parts of southern England and has long been a favourite in cottage gardens, is detested by moles who will not venture within thirty yards of it once the plant is established.

In recent years it has become standard practice on most farms to sow dressed seed-corn, and this takes an enormous toll of birds just at the time when the residents are feeding the first nestlings and the main stream of spring migrants are arriving. In this case, the poison used is a compound of organo-mercury, and it causes the miserable deaths of literally thousands of birds in arable areas.

Anyone who is prepared to be a nuisance, generally assumed to be a crack-pot and a scaremonger, and carry local conservancy beyond the confines of the garden, will find plenty of opportunities to campaign against a widespread attitude of total indifference to the plight of wild animals in the interests of short-term economy.

The problem of overhead cables is not one of economy ; in fact, it is quite the reverse, because every time a flock of birds, or a single large individual, flies into the wires between pylons, causing a short-circuit and local power failures, they cost money. Every year more and more cables are meshed across the countryside, particularly near estuaries working hydro-electric power-plants, where flocks of swans and waders find it increasingly hard to find a clear flight-way.

Corks and metal and plastic markers are used in some places to silhouette the wires, but these are technically troublesome ; an enlargement of the space allowed between the wires has been tried, with a resulting decrease in the accident rate ; and, no doubt, a complete solution will be found in the course of time, if only because the present situation is uneconomic.

Pollution of the high seas with fuel oil must end one day, too, and for the same reason ; the spraying of crops with toxic insecticides seems likely to continue for some time because its control would be largely only a matter of conscience.

I have, necessarily, shown the seamy side of country life as it is today and given a grim look at the future ; but there are signs that people are becoming concerned for the safety of our fauna, and when the novelty of the chemical and mechanical devices of civilisation has worn off, we may still be able to find a way to co-exist with wild animals.

For my part, although many of the casualties that I have handled have made me both sad and angry, I am grateful for the chances of knowing several hundred individual birds of some forty species ; enjoying the companionship of a swan, watching a ruff moult through its exotic breeding-plumage, and gaining the confidence of the wildest oceanic birds ; but, of all, the most rewarding moment is the sight of a once crippled bird taking to the air, fit and free to return to its natural life.

The few that remain permanently, occupying garden aviaries, are content enough and, with the advantage of security, develop in personality and intelligence to provide a constant source of fascinating study.

To my mind, pet-keeping in the accepted sense is a very dull and negative business, achieving nothing except perhaps an outlet for latent power-complexes ; but animal behaviour is a study still in its infancy, and offers scope for the amateur and an—otherwise much needed—excuse for confining wild animals.

INDEX

161